A Blood Stained Love

A Compilation of Authors

Copyright © 2021 From Pain to Purpose LLC

All rights reserved.

ISBN: 978-1-7367906-2-5

Blue Skies Are Going to Come After the Rain

Coretta J. Campbell

A Blood Stained love

The water could not have come fast enough, Katoria felt so dirty and ashamed. How did this happen? She felt lost. As the hot water dripped along her tainted skin, she replayed the sexual assault in her mind over and over. She scrubbed her skin so hard that she began to bleed. Every drop of water on her skin that cascaded over her could not erase what happened. She was just raped and violated.

As she stood in the shower with the water dripping over her she felt the urge to scream, but the scream did not come out. It reminded her of what had transpired a few hours ago and all she could do is let her tears fall and mix with the water from the shower.

When Katoria left the shower, she looked in the mirror, knowing at that moment her life would be forever changed. How did the person she liked and trusted the most become the person she hated? The thoughts overwhelmed her as she fell into the bed. She thought back to when she met Trey and how their friendship began.

It was a crisp fall day, Katoria was heading to her class. As she walked up to the door, she saw a gorgeous guy to her left. He was a vision of something she had never seen, and he had a smile for days. Katoria proceeded to enter the building and smiled to herself.

When she had a break during her class sessions, Katoria would often go to the cafeteria to grab a snack and would sit and talk with a few of her college friends. As luck would have it, he was in the cafeteria sitting by himself. Katoria, as the shy type, would not have taken it upon herself to say something to him. So, she just sat there staring into her teacup. The moment she finished her tea to throw away her trash she heard, "Excuse me, aren't you the girl I saw earlier?"

Katoria stated, "Yes, I am."

He said, "My name is Trey."

"Katoria," She extended her hand with a smile.

"Nice to meet you. What are you about to get into?" Trey started to pick up her books. "I have to get back to class." Katoria answered, shyly.

Trey bit his bottom lip as he asked to walk her to class. Katoria obliged and they made small talk as they walked across campus. When they finally reached the classroom, Trey asked her for her number. How could she deny him? He was being so sweet.

Later that evening when she returned home, Katoria picked up the phone to call Trey, but hung up the phone. She did not want to seem too eager. As soon as she hung up the phone, it rang. "Hello," Trey spoke on the other end of the phone.

Butterflies fluttered in the pit of her stomach. The sound of his voice made something inside of her feel easy. She smiled as they talked about their lives; past, present, and future. It seemed like she had known him forever; he made her feel comfortable. By the time they hung up, Katoria was imagining his arms around her and their lips entangled in a passionate kiss.

As the days went on, Katoria and Trey became good friends, they would spend their free time in the cafeteria talking about goals and their dreams. It was obvious they had a bond. Katoria did not want to establish any relationship with Trey because of all the hurt she had experienced in the past. The guys she met in the past were only interested in sex, and that was not what she wanted for herself in a relationship.

Despite the attraction she had to him, Katoria and

Trey did not have a romantic relationship. They were basically great friends. So, it took Katoria by surprise when Trey asked her to go out on a date. It was a Saturday night, and Trey picked up Katoria from her home. She was impressed by how great Trey looked. They had dinner at a fine Italian restaurant; the food and atmosphere were amazing. The night was young, so they decided to drive around the city. The night sky was glistening as the stars were in alignment.

Trey told Katoria to close her eyes, she was wondering where she was going and was in suspense. When they arrived, Trey said, "Katoria, we are here." When she opened her eyes, he led her into a building. They proceeded to enter the elevator and got out on the 6th floor. As they entered the apartment, Trey told her, "This my sis place, I'm just checking on it while she outta town."

"Oh really?" Katoria looked around. "You wouldn't be tryna get the draws?" She smirked. "Do I look like that type of guy?" Trey questioned as he disappeared into the back of the apartment. Katoria took a seat on the couch and thumped through the mail that sat on the end table. A couple of the letters had a woman's name on them, and others were addressed to Trey.

"Katoria!" She jumped when she heard him call her name. "Come here, baby." He said, sweetly.

Her eyebrows rose on her forehead and suddenly a chill covered her skin. Katoria's eyes darted from the backroom to the front door. She liked Trey but she was not ready to make things serious between them. Her mind was telling her to raise on up out of there. She had the perfect opportunity to leave the apartment, but Trey was a nice guy, and she didn't want to ruin their friendship. So, against her better judgement, she followed his voice to the bedroom. The television was blurring in the background as Trey sat on the edge of the bed. He reached out for her and reluctantly, she stepped into his arms.

"Trey," She said, looking down at him, "it's getting late. I have to get home to study for midterms."

Trey smiled at her, "You want to take a test? I have all the answers." He kissed her stomach.

Katoria pulled away. "For real, Trey. I have to go." She started to walk out of the room, but he quickly grabbed her arm. "Let go. You're hurting me."

"Com'on, baby. You know you want it. You came

here, looking good, smelling good." Trey pulled at her dress.

"I'm leaving." Katoria took one step forward before Trey grabbed her and tossed her on the bed.

Trey had taken her arms and pinned them down, she was fighting him with all her might, but he was too strong. All negative thoughts came to play as he began to tear at her clothes. Katoria was crying and pleading with him to stop, but he would not listen. Trey was acting like a wild animal that could not be tamed. He reached up under the bed and proceeded to put a gun against Katoria's head all while violating every inch of her soul. He forced her to do things she would've never done. What did I do? She questioned to herself as he pounded on her soul.

As the tears flowed, the fifteen minutes seemed like fifteen hours. Every thrust, every motion was ripping away her insides; this was hell. Katoria could not breathe.

After Trey finished humiliating her and taunting her, he then began to threaten her. Trey stated, "If you tell anyone they won't believe you, I will say you were willing." Katoria could not speak as she was numb, but those words stayed in her mind.

A Blood Stained love

"It's my fault... "It's my fault", Katoria stated in her mind. She felt like trash! How did she let this happen? She ran out of the building. People were staring at her. She remembered what her mother told her-- always carry money in case of emergencies. She ended up calling a cab to take her home.

It wasn't enough to process what had happened, to make matters worse, Trey kept calling her cell phone continuously leaving derogatory messages and threatening her to not tell anyone. How would she function seeing him in school?

The days turned into nights, the nights turned into weeks, weeks turned into months. Katoria was not herself. She had to change her cell phone number and avoided running into Trey at school. She was not herself; her aura was different. She was no longer the fun, bubbly person she once was. Her persona was withdrawn and sad. Her grades were beginning to suffer, and she was in a dark and cold place.

Katoria felt so alone because she could not tell anyone, and it was eating at her soul. Every day was a struggle and it showed.

A year went by and Katoria was moving along in slow motion. She knew that she had to put the incident behind her and move forward. She had thought about seeking therapy, but the shame and guilt would not let her do it, so she just pushed the memories aside.

As time went on, Katoria knew she had to move on. She graduated from college, but she did not attend the graduation, it was not in her to attend. She felt like her spirit could not take the thought of seeing Trey.

Katoria's career started to take off after she graduated. She was able to land a position at a prestigious marketing firm as Lead Marketing agent. The position was very demanding and allowed her to focus on work and not the past. Her workdays were an easy twelve hours not leaving much time for recreation.

One day while shopping at the local department store to buy makeup, she ran into the salesman who worked in the shoe department. He was nice looking and very charismatic. He smiled and she smiled back.

As she proceeded to leave the store, the gentleman said, "Excuse me, are you single?" Katoria thought that was very upfront and bold, she answered "Yes, single at the moment." He introduced himself to her as Byron, he gave her his number and she left.

Katoria held onto the number for weeks, as the fear of dating scared her. The thought of dating just made her feel sad. After about four weeks she called him. They had many nights of long conversations which made Katoria feel happy, it was nice to talk to someone for a change other than her dog.

After a few weeks of conversations Byron asked Katoria to go on a date. At first, she said yes, then she cancelled. Byron thought that was odd. Katoria decided that could do a day date and in the open, they decided on a picnic in the park.

It was there on the first date that Katoria explained to Byron what had happened to her a few years prior. Katoria knew it was different when Byron held her and comforted her that it was not her fault. All the hurt and pain inside her was released and it felt good to not feel like the victim. Katoria knew that it had come time to release the hurt and judgement of herself to begin to live again.

Katoria and Byron began to date exclusively. Their dates were not intimate but just getting to know each other by taking walks, going shopping, attending movies and dinners.

One day Katoria received an invitation to attend a classmate's wedding. She mentioned it to Byron, and it was a go. She was nervous and excited to attend the festivities and have a great time.

The wedding was held in September. It was a nice fall day. They decided just to attend the reception as the church was far from the venue. Katoria decided on a nice black dress and heels. Byron looked extra sharp in his suit. They made a great couple.

As they arrived at the venue, Katoria checked her makeup and hair to make sure she was okay. They then proceeded to enter the cocktail hour, where there were a magnitude of people waiting to eat their appetizers and cocktails.

Katoria saw and spoke to some of her fellow classmates from elementary school, everyone looked amazing.

After the cocktail hour, they went into the main dining area for the reception.

A Blood Stained love

The venue was beautiful with a lot of high-end décor which Katoria loved. She saw her classmate who got married and briefly waved and smiled. As Katoria went to sit at the assigned table with Byron as she looked out of the corner of her eye, she saw him. Trey! Katoria immediately started to feel ill and excused herself to the lady's room. When she entered the bathroom stall, she began to feel flushed, and the tears started flowing. Katoria had to leave and there was no way she could stay. When she got back to the table, she could feel Trey's eyes on her with a smirk on his face, it had been years since she last saw him.

Immediately, she told Byron they had to leave because something she ate earlier that did not agree with her stomach. Katoria gave the new bride and groom their envelope and explained that they could not stay.

On the way home, Katoria closed her eyes and all she saw was darkness and felt hurt again. How could this be? Out of all the places to see Trey, her friend's wedding. She could not tell Byron anything and just let it be.

This episode took Katoria back into her dark place. She decided to end the relationship with Byron, he was completely thrown off not understanding why it had to end.

Katoria became a recluse, her days were filled with work and her night filled with tears. She felt so alone. There were nights she didn't want to live.

A year after the incident. Katoria started a new job, the benefits were great, and the money was decent. Work was all she knew. Her friends wanted to take her out, go on trips but Katoria made excuses all the time.

Katoria had a friend named Natasha who always wanted to hang out. This evening Natasha invited her to a housewarming. Katoria decided to go, as they approached the building Katoria stopped and smiled. She needed to come and get some air. While at the housewarming they were in the kitchen talking with the older ladies. They provided many jokes and words of advice. One of the ladies, Ms. Lynn, was inquiring about Katoria's love life. She mentioned that she was seeing someone a year prior, but things didn't work out. Ms. Lynn provided some old school words of wisdom that made Katoria think and that night she decided to call Byron.

It was great to hear his voice and they caught up on things like they never lost touch. Katoria and Byron decided to have a date for dinner and a movie. When Byron picked up Katoria he looked more handsome than before.

As time went on, Katoria explained to Byron what transpired at the wedding previously. He was upset he felt Katoria should have told him. She explained she did not want to ruin her classmate's wedding day.

Byron became Katoria's protector and assured her that he would be there for her always to protect her. Katoria had to learn to love and trust again. Eventually after dating a few years, they became engaged and eventually married. Katoria knew that blue skies would come after the rain.

The End

A Blood Stained love

Incursion of a Goddess

M. Russell

A Blood Stained love

It was ten minutes past showtime, and I was sprinting down Champlain street in four-inch heels, sweat dripping down my temples, weaving through the bustling Adams Morgan crowds. I was stressing over arriving late. The event was an art showcase for a friend in D.C. at a small gallery she rented out for the evening. I saw the security standing before me at the entrance and halted to a stop as I approached the entrance. I was already late. As I drew closer to the guard, I calmed my nerves and wiped the sweat off the edge of my forehead.

"ID?" The tall guard asked sternly as he reached his hand out.

I smiled but said nothing. As I handed him my identification card, I caught a glimpse of the inside of the gallery as the couple ahead of me walked through the narrow, white door. The name of the gallery was painted on the windows in white letters, Corinto Gallery, it was small but had a nice vibe to it.

"Here you go, have fun," his deep voice almost sounded demanding.

To my surprise, the music was a variety of jazz and local Go-Go, the culture of the city setting the mood for the evening. There were so many paintings displayed along the walls that were beautifully painted by my friend, Rochelle. I reached for a champagne flute from the cocktail waitress and decided to start from the left and make my way through the showcase. Everyone's attention was focused on the masterpieces, so no one noticed my tardiness,

"What a relief!" I whispered

"Well, if it isn't our very own Jeni LeGon!"

I spun around smiling, "Rochelle!"

"Guys, this is my friend, the amazing tap dancer I was telling you about! Hey Thena!" Rochelle gave me a big embrace in excitement.

The two guys who were accompanying her looked interesting. Rochelle looked like a model in her strapless black dress with her long neck and flawless brown skin. She grabbed my hand as we stood there complimenting each other.

"Thena?" the guy with the beard asked.

"Well, it's Athena, you know, like the Greek goddess. But I call her Thena," she smiled.

"And I keep telling her to call me Chelle. Rochelle is so formal," she told them as she playfully rolled her eyes.

We all laughed, "Girl, your work is amazing, I knew you were talented but wow!"

"Talent, recognizes talent," she said and winked.

We spent the next hour exploring the showcase and discussing her art in between people greeting her and thanking her for the invite. I drank two more glasses of champagne and ate a few spring rolls. . As the event was nearing the end, it was time for Rochelle to make her keynote speech. I glanced around the room at the crowd slowly making their way to her and decided to slip away to use the bathroom. I stood in front of the mirror and freshened up. My blue dress hugged my curves while my tight curls sat perfectly on the sides of my face.

I started to feel the effects of the bubbly from earlier. I stumbled out of the bathroom and held my trembling hands out grasping for the dingy walls to guide me where it was her time to shine. I thought I was a heavyweight when it came to alcohol- boy was I wrong! As I followed Rochelle's growing voice, I unexpectedly bumped into someone.

"Watch where you're going!" the tall stranger said.

I looked up at him and apologized. He was handsome with strong cheekbones and shaggy curls that sat on the top of his head. His frown immediately turned into a smile when he looked down at me.

"Oh, excuse me, I apologize for my tone," he didn't look away from my eyes.

I blushed, "No the apology is all mine. Take care," I said as I moved past him and back into the crowd.

Rochelle was reflecting on her history as an artist and began discussing what incident brought upon the vision she had for this showcase. She acknowledged me from a distance when she spotted me in the sea of people while delivering her speech.

"Excuse me, but could I stand next to you?" a low voice whispered.

I stayed silent as I turned to look and saw that it was the man I bumped into earlier. I rolled my eyes and tried to put my focus back on to Rochelle.

"My name is Joe, by the way. What's your name?" he turned to face me.

I ignored him and tried to stabilize my balance because it felt like I was rocking back and forth. The heels weren't helping, they provided no support. I could feel him still staring at me and waiting for my name, but he wasn't my focus now.

"Oh, am I bothering you?"

I turned to face him and whispered as aggressively as I could, "Actually yes, I am trying to listen to her speech, and you keep talking!" I said rolling my eyes

"Oh, my bad."

He sucked his teeth as I turned my attention back to Rochelle. The alcohol got the best of me and I tripped and fell right into his strong arms. He brought me back to my feet slowly and suggested that he mov me to a bench that was placed off to the side and away from the crowd. I gave in and followed his lead and sat down because I didn't feel stable in my heels. One of the cocktail waitresses came over with a glass of water for me and I almost died of embarrassment.

"Athena," I said in between sips.

"What?"

"My name is Athena."

"So, I'm in the presence of a goddess!" he flashed his pearly smile.

I smiled *"He is cute. I am not sure why I'm being so rude to him."*

"So, Goddess, are you good? Do you want to sit for a while and sober up? I could sit with you and keep you company," he grabbed my hand.

I inhaled the scent of his sweet cologne, wow, it has been so long since a man came this close to me while flirting. Me running from one dance class to the next didn't give them much time to say hello. I have to admit I am enjoying this attention.

"What?" He asked with a straight face.

I looked up at him, "Huh?"

"You're staring at me."

"You look good, and you smell good, I'm just admiring it."

He laughed, "Umm okay, are you sure you're good?"

A wave of embarrassment came over me. Did I read this wrong? Was he not flirting with me? *Oh God!* I leaned forward and grabbed another glass of champagne from the tray moving past us again and took a few sips trying to hide my face behind the glass.

"Oh, so the party is still going on, yea?"

"I'm sorry but I've embarrassed myself enough tonight. You don't have to babysit me," I lowered my head and looked away.

"I'm not babysitting. I'm sitting with a goddess."

I paused with a bewildered look, "So…am I reading this wrong or am I right?"

"You're definitely right, I'm into you. Are you single?"

"Yes," unintentionally blurted it out.

"Good. You are beautiful. Your mama should've named you Aphrodite."

"Oh, so you're familiar with Greek Mythology?"

"Just a little. I'm a poet, there are certain subjects that stick with us to help our creativity. I mean, you will hear plenty of poets talk about how someone or something is their muse. That word is commonly mentioned in Greek Mythology."

"Oh wow, okay," I said putting my glass down on the counter behind us.

"What about you? Are you an artist of some sort?"

"A dancer."

"Ah, I should've known by those legs," he leaned in close to my neck as he spoke.

Chills rushed over me; he did smell good. I could tell that he sensed I didn't want to answer because he leaned back and reached his arm behind me resting it on the counter next to my drink.

"What kind of dancer are you? Hip hop?"

"No, no. I am trained in ballet, but my specialty is tap. I love everything about tap dance. I atake some classes that incorporate hip hop style into tap dance to bring a more modern flare to it!"

"You sound so excited explaining it to me. It must be your passion," he scooted closer to me.

"Y-yes, it is," my voice shook a little. I could almost feel the grip of his hands on my curves, it's been so long.

"I could tell," he said, breaking me out of my thoughts.

I turned my body and grabbed my glass and downed the rest. No point in sipping it. I was about to let my inhibitions go and have this man tonight.

Turning to face him I started, "Hey what are

you- "

"Thena! Thank you so much for coming girl! We gotta hang out soon, when it's not so formal," Rochelle pulled me up into a hug, "Are you good? I see you met Joe."

"I did," I winked at her.

"Miss Rochelle, always a pleasure," he leaned in for a handshake.

She gave a hug instead and pulled back, "You better be taking care of my girl here!"

"I am."

"Good," she turned back to me, "Well the showcase is over. Do you need a ride back home?"

"Oh," I did not even think about getting back home.

"I could take you home, if you'd like," Joe offered; we exchanged looks.

"Yeah, that'll be nice."

Rochelle and I exchanged smiles, "Uh oh, let me find out you two have a love connection. You know I'll take all the credit during my speech at your wedding, right?"

We laughed.

"Girl, bye!" I laughed waving her off.

"Later girl," Rochelle hugged me again before turning to say goodbye to her other guests.

I sat back down and then felt his hand rub against the side of my arm and I almost melted. I know I just met him, and I didn't expect this to go further than tonight but he seems nice, and I need a stress reliever. I looked up at his eyes so I could read him.

He is interested and seems safe enough. I'll hang out a little longer and see where this goes with him. Oh, he is smiling now. Now I'm smiling, ugh. I have dance class in the morning, but I should be okay.

"So, where to next, Goddess?"

"Would you stop calling me that?"

"Why? Your name is literally Athena and you look like a Goddess in that dress," he checked me out as he reached his hand out for me.

"Oh lord." I blushed and reached my hand out and put it in his and stood up. *Woah, the room is spinning.* I laid my hand over my eyes and tried to focus.

"Are you okay?" he asked.

"Just give me a minute," I could feel the dizziness calming, "too much champagne, went to my head," I nervously chuckled.

I've never felt that while drinking before. I shook it off and drank the remainder of my water that I had put to the side for that extra glass of champagne. I looked up and Joe was standing there smiling, patiently waiting for me to get myself together.

"Are you sure you're okay? Would you like me to take you home?"

"Yes, I'm fine now. Thanks for asking," I grabbed his hand for support.

"Maybe you need some real food. At this time of the night the only thing open is carry out.. Would that work?"

"Sure. I want chicken wings and fries with

mambo sauce smothered over it?"

He laughed, "Well, I live on this side of the city. We can order and take it back to my place and chill out. But no more drinks. I think you've had enough," he winked.

"I agree. Plus, I have practice in the morning," we headed for the door.

He paused and turned to face me, "Jeni LeGon, I get it now!" he laughed as he opened the door for me.

"You heard that earlier?"

"Yes. I wasn't too far away when I saw Rochelle approach the prettiest woman in the room," I blushed.

We were walking down the street with my arm in his talking about our lives and interests. I felt comfortable with Joe even though we just met. He had me go inside the carryout to grab the food so I wouldn't be standing outside alone at one o'clock in the morning. The same dizzy spell rushed over me briefly while they were handing me our food, but I decided against telling him. I wanted to enjoy the rest of the night; I didn't want this man to think I couldn't hold my liquor.

A fifteen-minute walk across a few blocks and we finally approached his apartment. I followed him through the lobby to the elevator hall and waited until one opened. The next thing I knew we were standing in the elevator, Joe pressed up against me and I'm holding his jacket. Did I just pass out?

"Joe?"

"Yea?"

"Never mind," I kept my thoughts to myself and we began to kiss.

What is going on with me tonight? Am I just tired? I'll have to remember to ask Rochelle what brand of champagne that was because I'm having some serious side effects.

Ding.

The elevator doors opened to the 7th floor, "Come on," he led me down the hall. Suddenly my heart started to race, and I felt a little dizzy again.

"I live alone, so don't worry about anyone else being here."

The door opened and I looked inside. It was clean and neat, designed by a man. I felt Joe put his hand on my chin and lift it.

"You okay, Goddess?"

"It's Athena. And yes. Let's go inside and eat," I forced a smile.

The dizziness faded again as I was eating. Maybe I just needed to eat.

"Wake up, wake up," Joe was liftin me up from my plate.

Everything was foggy, "I fell asleep again?"

"Yeah, uh…do you have narcolepsy or something that I need to know about?"

"What? No! This is strange," I'm in my head now. *Why on earth do I keep passing out like this?*

"Well go to the bathroom and get cleaned up, you fell right down on your plate."

"Oh my god, please tell me I didn't," I felt mortified.

He just laughed and pointed to the bathroom.

I went in and closed the door. Holy shit. I have mambo sauce across my face. I don't even feel drunk at this point, just lightheaded. I cleaned up my face then used the bathroom. As I was washing my hands, I heard a knock on the door.

"You okay?"

I turned around and opened the door, "Yes."

"I'm sorry to laugh but I have never seen someone drop on their plate like that before!"

I rolled my eyes and stepped close to him.

He didn't say anything, he just grabbed the sides of my arms and laid his face close to mine. Our bodies were so close I could feel his excitement. He gently pushed me back to the sink and opened the slit in my dress as he slid his hand up my thigh. I softly bit his ear and rubbed my hands up his arms and rested them on the back of his neck.

"Do you give your consent?"

"What? Are you serious?!?"

He pulled back and looked me in my eyes, "Seriously."

I felt a heavy wave of exhaustion over my entire body, but I was feeling this moment, so I pushed past it and grabbed him.

"Yes, I give consent," I slurred as I blindly reached out to him.

"Thank you," he said; I closed my eyes as he began lifting my dress.

***

The sun aggressively beamed through my eyelids. As I squinted my eyes tight to shade the brightness, I felt my entire body heavy like I got hit by a truck. I tried to say Joe's name but all I could make out was a faint mumble. What the hell was in that champagne? I've never been this out of it before, wait… was I drugged? There's no way a few glasses of champagne would have my body in pain like this.

I force my heavy head up and open my eyes a little. It felt like a ton of bricks were on my chest as I struggled to sit up. That hurts, I looked down and saw a huge bruise on my inner thighs. Instantly my skin crawled and the hairs on my arms and back stood up. Something's not right. It took all the strength I had to move to the edge of the bed when I heard a grunt.

My head whipped around and saw Joe laying on the opposite side of the bed, asleep in peace. What did he do to me? I swung my legs to the edge of the bed to prepare to stand up, but I felt sluggish. I hear soft breathing coming from underneath me, so I slowly looked down and my heart sunk. To my shock there laid a second man, naked and I became nauseous.

Did he touch me? Why was he naked? I wanted to wake Joe, but my thoughts halted me. Did he set me up?

I took any strength in me and hopped over the stranger. My heart raced as I gathered my clothes that were strung across the bedroom. I snuck out of the bedroom and quickly dressed in the living room. My entire body was in pain as I desperately looked around the room for my purse and heels. It felt like I was searching forever, I was so scared they were going to wake up. Finally, I spotted my things and I grabbed them rushing to the front door as silently as possible when I heard the toilet flush from the bathroom. I froze in fear and just stood there with my hand on the doorknob listening.

"Aye, man. That bitch left already?" the third man

asked.

My eyes grew wide, and it seemed like my heartbeat was loud across the apartment; I was going to get caught. I held my breath before rushing out of the apartment and quietly closed the door behind me. I looked in both directions, but I didn't recognize anything. I ran down the longer part of the hallway where I saw signs for the elevator and stairs. My vision was blurry, and I don't think I took a breath during that long run down the hall, but I made it to the elevator fast. 7th floor, but it's coming from the 15th floor, my body shook. I couldn't just stand there waiting I was going to get caught! I ran through the stairway door, still barefoot, and raced down the stairs. By the time I got the 3rd level I fell into the wall and finally exhaled. I heard a door close from an upper level which jolted me up and I continued to run down the stairs until I reached the lobby and ran outside.

I continued running down the busy streets with no real direction until I came up on Pleasant Pops, a corner coffee shop I used to go to with my dad when I went to school at Duke Ellington. I slipped in quickly and watched the windows to see if anyone was running after me, but no one was running at all. He set me up to be raped! My adrenaline subsided allowing my body to feel every bit of pain from what they did to me. My body started to tremble, and I find it hard to breathe. I went to get my phone from my purse to call my dad, but sound became distant, my vision overpowered by darkness and I passed out.

* * *

My eyes open slowly…bright lights…pain.

Beep, beep.

I hear faded voices, figures hovering over me, a dark silhouette making a noise, but I can't quite make out what they are saying.

Beep, beep.

"Honey, Honey! Do you know where you are?"

Finally, a voice. As all other sounds started coming back to my hearing the fog in my vision cleared up. A doctor is leaning over me while the nurse is checking my vitals. I took notice that these professional black women complimented their uniforms with their personal fashion, it was beautifully distracting.

I felt her cold hands touch my leg and I jumped. A flashback of those guys holding my legs down just invaded my mind and I could hear Joe's laugh asking who is next. I squeeze my eyes closed.

"I want to get some scans and blood work done to make sure there aren't any serious underlying problems," Her faded voice explaining.

"No! No, I'm fine. I just want to go home!"

I felt a rush of shame and guilt. I was raped but had it not been for me going home with a stranger I wouldn't have been in this predicament. It's my fault.

I heard a deep voice getting closer to my triage room when the door opened.

"Okay, someone ordered for blood work?"

I saw a tall man standing before me and instinctively grabbed the nurse's wrist and held on tight as I freaked out. My body trembled with fear and for the first time I cried.

"Okay, thank you. We'll take it from here," The doctor said as she stepped in between me and the phlebotomist.

He looked confused, "Umm they sent me here, triage 8, and told me to draw blood samples."

"And I said I got it," she looked back at my trembling body, "We have to run a few more tests so we'll just take care of this. Thank you!"

He grunted and threw his hands up, "Fine. Just be sure to follow through till the end. I'll move on to the next patient."

After he left the doctor closed the door again and looked at me.

"Okay, sweetie. It is just the three of us. I'm Doctor Watson and this is Nurse Desirée. We're here to help but we need to know exactly what's hurting you," she said calmly as she and the nurse exchanged looks.

I continued to cry.

"Honey, I'm here to help," as she stepped closer, "You're hurt, and we can help. What is your name?"

I stared in her eyes terrified. I just wanted to go home and hide and forget this all happened.

Her tone lowered and sounded as sweet as love, "Honey, please let us help you. What's your name?"

The nurse stroked the top of my hand with her fingers. I looked down at it. I didn't realize I was still holding on to her. I felt like my body froze, I could not move and all I felt was pain. I looked at the two of them and they are watching me with the looks of concern and compassion.

I closed my eyes and winced in pain, "Ah-theen-"

My body couldn't stop shaking.

"Atheen is your name?" the nurse asked.

"N-No," I swallowed a gulp of my own saliva, and squeezed my eyes tight, "Athena."

"Athena, good job. Now can you show us all of the places your body hurts?"

I knew the pain was resonating in several parts of my body, but I don't think any of us were prepared for what we saw. Large bruises and scratch marks from my knees trailing up my thighs and a deep purple bruise on my hip.

The nurse said in shock. I looked up at her, she had tears forming in her eyes as she looked at me then at the doctor. I saw the doctor gulp and take a deep breath before looking away from my legs.

"Okay Desirée, I need you to rush an order for blood work and scans. We have to make sure there isn't internal damage," she told the nurse as she carefully laid the hospital gown on me.

They were talking amongst themselves and it felt like time stood still and their voices were distant again. Every time I felt movement around me my skin crawled. *How could they rape me? What did they do to me? Joe set me up, but why me?* The questions were endless but, I am to blame. I went home with a stranger and put myself in this situation.

"Is there anyone we can call for you?"

I thought of my dad, he lives on the other side of D.C. and he would come here faster than they could hang up the line, but I don't want him to see me like this. It has just him and I since my mother died.

"My friend Rochelle," my words stuttered. I don't want her to blame herself for this because she knew him, but I need my friend here. I opened my phone and gave it to the nurse then she left to call Rochelle for me.

"Okay Athena, listen to me. I need you to take a few deep breaths and focus," Dr. Watson said as she checked my pulse.

"Could you tell us what happened? We can get a better understanding of how to treat you if we know who caused these injuries."

The nurse slipped back in, handed me the phone letting me know Rochelle was on the way.

"I-I," I couldn't get the words out.

"Did someone hurt you Athena?"

I nodded my head. They explained to me that if I did a rape kit, I did not have to file a report immediately and at least the evidence would be available for when I am ready, but I was confused and unsure if I wanted to do a kit. About an hour later Rochelle ran in the room and cried while she hugged me. She apologized over and over for letting me leave without her.

"What happened Thena? Oh my God, look at

you!" she cried as she stroked my hair, "what happened after we left each other?"

I explained to her what Joe did to me and explained how I was to blame for even being in that situation.

"Absolutely not! You went home with Joe; you didn't know those other guys were there! This is not your fault! Joe took advantage of you and you deserve to take your power back! I'll be here with you but please Thena, please do the rape kit so we could put that asshole in jail! Him and his friends," she started to cry again, "I'm so sorry, I'm so sorry I would've never let you leave with him!"

"Please don't blame yourself, neither one of us could've known this would happen," I started to cry along with her. I just couldn't shake the guilt. He drew me in so easily with his smooth words. It was like he knew how lonely I was; I was ripe for the picking. I did not stand a chance against him.

I agreed and signed the papers. The doctor did the rape kit step by step, trying to comfort me along the way. With every touch against my skin, I got a flashback from the night before. Horrible images appeared like scenes from a movie, and it felt surreal. I couldn't believe this was happening to me.

I squeezed Rochelle's hand tight and exhaled, "This is gonna be a lot for me to say," I turned my attention towards Dr. Watson, "Can we bring the police in here to take the report? I'd rather not keep repeating myself."

"Oh my God Athena! What happened?" the tears continued to flow down her face.

Dr. Watson left for fifteen minutes then returned with two police officers. The woman officer was taking my report while the male officer was off to the side getting the information from the medical staff. The whole time Rochelle was crying and rubbing my shoulder as she stood beside me holding my hand.

"Ma'am, we will need to take pictures for evidence," the woman officer announced.

I started to panic. This was getting too real, and I couldn't believe that I did this to myself.

"This is all my fault!"

"What?" Rochelle and the officer both asked.

"I left with him! I went home with him! I started having sex with him!" I was choking on my words as I cried out, I could feel the pain of the bruises.

"Miss Athena, this was not consensual. It may have started out consensual between you and the individual but as soon as you passed out there was no more consent. Not to mention you did not consent to the two other individuals."

"Did they run a tox screen?" Rochelle asked me.

I shrugged my shoulders; I don't know what that consists of and I don't know for what.

"Yes, we did, we suspected a date rape may have happened," Dr. Watson responded toward the officer, not Rochelle.

Oh. Oh my god.

I looked around the room at everyone watching me struggle through the rest of my statement. I felt like their eyes were judging me even though they were saying supportive affirmations. Rochelle finally stopped crying enough to pull it together to give the police all the information that she knew on Joe. She didn't know much outside of his name and number and mentioned how she wasn't sure if Joe was his real name or if it was short for something. My skin crawled hearing her mention his name.

"Thena, stop!"

I looked down and saw blood dripping from my arm. I didn't realize that I was scratching myself.

"Oh, I'm… I didn't realize. I need to take a shower, I can still feel them all over me," I closed my eyes.

The night before had some gaps in my memory, probably because there was a drug slipped into my drink. I can't remember much but I could still feel everything as if it were happening.

"Let's call psych in here," I heard the doctor order.

"What? No, I'm fine I just need to shower. I just need to-," it felt like my throat grew extremely dry and I felt like I was choking. I grabbed my neck and threw my head back gasping.

"Someone please helps her!"

"She's having a panic attack, please move aside Rochelle so we can help your friend."

I watched as Nurse Desirée moved Rochelle over so Doctor Watson could get close to help. I heard a deep voice and went into a full panic trying to rip the IV out of my arm. I felt like I was out of my mind, I couldn't control the fear that was overpowering me mentally.

"Don't go all Girl, Interrupted Daisy on me before they take you away! Get it together, please!" Rochelle begged.

"Look at me, look at me! You are safe! Listen to the sound of my voice Athena, it is 10:36am on Monday morning," Doctor Watson started circling her finger on my palm, "you are safe, you are here at the hospital."

My eyes opened gradually. That calmed me down and I was able to realize that it was the police officer who I heard. Rochelle was in the corner hugging on the nurse crying, scared of what was going to happen to me. I don't want to be locked up in a crazy house, I thought as I forced myself to calm down before they sent me up.

"We are all very proud of you for being brave in doing the kit and giving your statement, now it's time for you to take care of yourself," Doctor Watson said.

"Athena, we have your statement and the kit. We're going to leave you to heal, take care of yourself, we'll be in touch for the investigation," the police officers said as they were exiting the room.

A short woman came in behind them with two men in a white scrub. I twisted my hand and held Doctor Watson's and looked at her helplessly.

"Please don't let them take me away," I whispered to her.

"Are you good?" she whispered back. I nodded yes.

She turned her attention towards the workers from the mental health department, "Thank you but all of that is not necessary, I ordered for someone to come down to help give Miss Wilson some coping tools and a follow up appointment."

"Oh, okay," the short lady sent the men away and turned back towards me, "Hi there. You are very brave, and we are all here to support you. May I sit with you awhile to talk so I could give you tools you'll need once you're discharged?"

I nodded my head.

Rochelle gave me a hug, "I got your back girl. I'll be right outside your door!"

The nurse and doctor both followed Rochelle out of the room leaving me to this new doctor.

"You may ask me anything or talk to me about anything that's on your mind. When we're done, we'll schedule a follow up appointment so I could see you within a week before I refer you to an outside office," I took a deep breath as I listened to her words, "This is the first step to your healing. Are you ready?"

I nodded my head and prepared for the most uncomfortable moment of this woman trespassing in my brain and helping me fit the pieces back together like a puzzle. One night of poor decisions created a life tainted and unrecognized. I looked at the window watching the rain tap against the glass and wondered will I ever be able to tap my way through life carefree again. I will never be the same, the price I have to pay will be unforgiving with an end date undetermined.

A Blood Stained love

A Deadly Crush

T.B. Scott

A Blood Stained Love

Tamara stared in the mirror looking at her face. What was once a thing of beauty, was now a face of horror. Tamara was 4'10", nice slim build. She rocked different colored wigs and her complexion, was as dark as the evening sky. She had nice full lips, with bedroom eyes. But today, they were swollen with bruised eyes. At just 15 years old, she never expected to be in the position she was currently in. Her first boyfriend, the boy she gave her heart to, turned out to be her nightmare. She could not stand to look at her reflection. For it was a reminder of what her Mom told her. Her Mom had her suspicions about her little boyfriend. She tried to warn Tamara, but Tamara swore she was in love. Her Mom often asked her what she knew about love at the age of 15. Tamara just swore she knew. You could not tell her anything. She just knew Tyrin was the boy for her. All the girls had a thing for him. Tyrin was 5'6" with a nice little slim cut built for him. Dark skin as well with a wavy Caesar haircut. He had a money sign tattoo on his neck. With that whole bad boy image going on, that all the girls at Martin Luther King High School loved. She thought she was special when he chose to be with her over all the

A Blood Stained love

other girls. She just knew she was the shit. Tamara was not the baddest chick there was, she was pleasing to the eye. Tamara was not your typical Philly chick. Tamara had that Philly chick attitude, at the same time, Tamara had a heart of gold also. She cried to herself as she slid down the wall onto her bathroom floor. She knew she could not let her Mom see her like this. Not that she really had a choice. It was no way Tamara could hide a busted bloody lip, with her eyes damn their swollen shut. This was the time she wished her brother, Jason, were home. Jason is doing a five-year bid for a gun charge.

At 18, her brother was already behind the 8ball. As far as their Dad, her and her Brother never knew their Dad. Their Mom didn't even really know who their Father was. She got around so often that truth be told, anybody could have been the Father of her and her Brother Jason. But she figured. Jason had a different father because Tamara and Jason did not really resemble one another. Only thing they had in common, was the fact that they both came out the same pussy. She wished this weren't her life. She just wanted this to be one of those nightmares that would be over. If she just opened her eyes. That was part of her problem. She kept her eyes closed to his bullshit. Now here she was, crying her eyes out on the bathroom floor next to the tub. But not just because of the abuse she experienced.

It was also due to how it ended that worried her the most. As she cries her heart out, she thinks back.

to how it started, and where it went wrong, and how it ended.

Five days ago

The first day of school was here and everybody was excited to be back. Truth be told, the first.

and the last day were the two best days of school. The days and months in between were up for debate.

Tamara was excited to see some of her classmates she went to Middle School with.

She sees her best friend Tracy running towards her, with her arms open for a hug. They embrace in a

big hug like they have not seen each other in years. When truthfully, they just saw each other.

Two days ago, at Tracy's Mom birthday party

"We're finally in High School. Moving up in the

world. I can't wait to see what this year brings.

No more dealing with these little junior high niggas. Now we can finally find some real men." Tracy says, surveying the scene as she addresses Tamara.

Tamara really wasn't that into meeting guys just yet. She was very much into her books. Matter of fact, she was still a virgin. Seeing her Mom always having different niggas over, made Tamara.

realize that, hoe life, was not the life for her.

"I don't know about hooking up with anybody just yet. I just wanna get through this school year first.

There will always be plenty of time for boys." Tamara says.

Tracy looked at her friend like she was weird. She just wanted Tamara to ease up some.

Enjoy life, stop being so much of a nerd.

"We got four years stuck in books. My Mom told me to enjoy High School. She said,

High School was the best four years of her life. I am

trying to experience that same feeling.

We're damn near grown now. Let's have some fun." Tracy says.

Tamara had a big goofy smile on her face. She and Tracy were like sisters. But Tracy could

be a little wild at times, as opposed to Tamara who was more the reserve type. But she could

be feisty when she had to be.

"Yooo, check them two niggas out. Damn, I'm trying to see what's up with them." Tracy's say's

as she spots Tyrin and some dude he was talking to.

"Look at you. School hasn't even started yet, and already, you're ready to pounce on some.

dick. Besides, he looks like he could be a junior or senior. You need to slow down. You don't

even know if he got a girl or not. You need to chill." Tamara says, hoping to be the voice of reason.

"Girl you need to cut it the fuck out, I'm just saying, loosen up some, live life." Tracy says.

Tyrin and his boy see Tamara and Tracy and start walking towards them. Tracy notices that they're

heading their way. She was getting a little hot in the pants as she checked Tyrin out. She thought,

his friend was cute, but Tyrin was the one she had her eyes on.

"Don't look now, but they're coming towards us." Tracy says.

"What's up with y'all? Me and my mans was checking y'all out. Y'all look good as shit. I'm Tyrin. This is my boy Sean." Tyrin says, doing the introductions.

Tracy was quick to spill her info before Tamara could even respond.

"I'm Tracy, nice to meet you."

Tyrin gave her a little head nod, as his eyes were focused on Tamara.

"What's up with your friend? She shy or something? She doesn't talk?" Tyrin ask, looking at Tamara like she was a home cooked meal.

Tracy gave her a nudge. Tamara was not sure if she wanted to give her name out so fast.

So, Tracy spoke up for her instead.

"Sorry about that. This is my rude friend Tamara. I don't know why she's acting all shy and shit.

This isn't like her."

Tamara looked at Tracy like she wanted to cuss her out. But for the mean time she went along with the conversation.

"Tamara huh? Nice to meet you." Tyrin says, extending his hand.

She thought for a second if she wanted to shake his hand or not. Tracy shook his hand first, then shook, Sean's hand. Tamara hated how thirsty her friend was acting. She finally shook both of their hands.

Tyrin seemed more interested in Tamara than he did Tracy.

"So how old are y'all?" Tracy asked.

A Blood Stained love

Sean finally spoke up as his eyes were glued to Tracy. Sean was 5'8 with a build like a middleweight boxer. Both Sean and Tyrin were on the wrestling team.

"I'm 17," Sean responds.

"I'm 16, but I will be 17 in four days. Matter of fact, I'm having a party for my birthday. Y'all should pull up. I got a DJ coming and everything."

Tamara remained quiet. She wasn't sure if she really wanted to hook up with any upperclassmen.

"So y'all are juniors?" Tracy asked.

Tyrin and Sean both replied "Yeah."

"I can tell they're freshmen." Sean says, with a sneaky smile on his face.

Sean had yet to take his eyes off Tracy's 5'0" thick build. She was already top and bottom heavy.

She had a grown woman's body that got her a lot of attention. She was dark brownskin.

People thought she was Japanese, because of her eyes. She was a niggas dream.

"I don't know about all of that. We just met y'all, we don't really know you. But thanks for the invite. Maybe some other time."

Tyrin was intrigued by the shy girl in front of him. She was his type, beautiful and reserved. It was no way he was going to let her slip through his fingers.

"What are you scared of? Your mom doesn't like you hanging out with older kids? She doesn't like you being around boys. Everything is cool. You got nothing to worry about." Tyrin says, trying to ease her nerves.

Tracy pulls Tamara to the side, trying to convince her to do it.

"What the fuck are you doing? You need to stop acting like a little girl. Have some fun for once.

What could it hurt to go to one party? You know it will be people there we know. Stop acting all stuck up."

Tyrin and Sean kept their eyes on Tamara and Tracy. Seconds later the girls came back to accept.

The invitation to the party.

"I look forward to seeing you. It was nice meeting

you both." Tyrin says, as he and Sean walked off. Tamara and Tracy had a gang of eyes on them from some of the other girls. Many of them were juniors and seniors, wondering how did these two manage to get Tyrin's attention. The hate was real and overflowing.

Two days later

Tyrin always seemed to pop up wherever Tamara was. It was almost as if he was stalking her. He managed to run into her at the Fresh Grocer in Sommerville. She was doing some classwork in their dining area. He walked up to her catching her off guard.

"Something about a smart girl that I love." He says, startling her.

He thought it was a little funny, and cute while she was startled.

"My bad, I didn't mean to scare you. I was just passing through. Happened to see you sitting here.

You mind if I join you?"

Tamara thought about it for a second before she agreed to let him join her. She didn't know what it was about him. But she was somewhat nervous but intrigued by him.

"Let me ask you something. How is it you always seem to pop up everywhere I be?"

Tyrin gazed out the window thinking of an answer he could give her. The last thing he wanted; was for her to think he was some kind of weird ass dude.

"I guess it's one of those things. We must be meant to be. Coincidence I guess you could say. But now, that we are talking. I wanna know, what's good with ya? You got somebody that you are fucking with or nah?"

She admired his direct to the point approach. She didn't like guys who beat around the bush.

"Nope, nobody I'm seeing or feeling. I got my mind on these books. The last thing that I need is to be distracted by boys. Tell me about you. Ain't no way you're gonna get me to believe that you ain't got a couple broads that you are out here smashin'. Ever since the day we met, bitches been giving me the evil eye." She says laughing.

Tyrin had a little smile on his face. He loved her smile.

"Honestly, yeah I smashed a couple broads. Being on the wrestling team, I got my fair share of groupies. But on some real shit, those broads ain't about nothing. Those broads are for everybody. I only smashed like two or three in all the time I been here."

Tamara didn't believe shit he was saying, but she was kind of digging him.

"Yeah right. You expect me to believe that, as good looking as you are, that you only smashed a couple broads? Nigga please, who the fuck you think you're talking to? Just keep that shit real my nigg. You ain't gotta bullshit me."

He loved this side of Tamara. She was acting all shy and shit when he met her. Now it's like Tamara's whole personality switched and he loved it.

"I knew that shy girl shit was an act. I knew it." He says, with a big smile on his face.

"No, it wasn't an act. I'm not shy either. I just know when a nigga is trying to bullshit me.

I'm a straight up type of chick. So, if you're gonna talk, then just keep that shit a million with me my nigga. Do that for me and I will do that for you."

A Blood Stained Love

Tyrin felt like he was in love. He also knew Tamara was gonna be a special kind of challenge. He was up for whatever challenge she was gonna possess.

Tyrin's Birthday Party

The basement in Tyrin's house was packed with teenagers. It was like one of those old school basement parties, niggas everywhere, and that one window that wouldn't open for shit. It wasn't just the

the basement that was crowded, but so was the living room and porch area. It seems like half the block and school were here. All that you smelled was weed. Tyrin was looking for Tamara. She said she had to use the bathroom. That was five minutes ago. He started making his way up the basement stairs to look for her. They had been getting really serious since they met. In her eyes they were a couple. But in his eyes, he told her whatever she wanted to believe, as long it would get him the pussy. He sees her on the porch talking to some dude name Kevin. Kevin was some random nut ass boy from his block. He doesn't even know who invited the nigga. Either way, that was neither here nor there. He was a little pissed that Tamara said she had to go

A Blood Stained love

to the bathroom, but here she is, on the porch talking to this Kevin nigga. He bumps past people walking to the porch. He was high on weed and drunk off Henny. His Mom knew the kids were getting drunk. She didn't care, as long as they didn't cause a scene. The other parents that we're here knew as well. All was good, as long as all stayed good.

Tyrin walks right up on Tamara and Kevin's conversation.

"So, here you are, I've been looking for you. I thought you said you had to go to the bathroom."

Tamara sensed something was up, but she wasn't really sure. Kevin was so high that he didn't really pay any attention.

"Yo, let me holla at you really quick." He says gently grabbing her, as to not bring attention to himself.

"Are you okay? What is wrong?" She asked.

Tyrin remained quiet as he pushed his way through people on his way upstairs to his bedroom.

Tamara saw Tracy on the couch sitting on Sean's lap, while another guy was rubbing on her arms and neck. She knew Tracy was fucked up, so she knew her friend would be of no help to her. She tried to reason with Tyrin again as they made it to the top floor.

'What is wrong? Why are you so quiet?"

Tyrin said nothing as they walked into his room. He tossed her towards his bed, causing her to fall on it. He shut the door behind him, then cut the lights on. The music was so loud, along with the noise from everybody here, that nobody would hear a thing coming from his room.

He looks at her with this real deranged look in his eyes. Tamara could feel her heart damn near pumping out of her chest. Terrified would hardly be the word to describe how she is feeling at this point.

"So, you're trying to play me at my own party. Why the fuck were you talking to that nigga?

You thought you was gonna holla at him and me?"

Tamara thought Tyrin was losing it. She figured he had to be fucked up thinking like this.

"What are you talking about? I did go to the bathroom. When I came out, I decided to get some air for a minute. He knows you're my man. It wasn't even like that. I talked to your mom just before he came on the porch."

Hearing his mom being mentioned really pissed Tyrin off.

"Don't bring my mom into your fucking lies. That nigga was trying to fuck you, wasn't he?"

Tamara got up and tried to walk past him, but Tyrin wasn't having it. He grabbed her by both of her arms and squeezed really hard.

"Bitch, did I say we're done? Did I say you could leave? Answer the question bitch. Were you planning on fucking him behind my back?"

Tamara knew things were officially going left at this point. She quietly prayed to God to get her out of this situation she was currently in. She tried to free herself from his grip, but he was too strong for her. He pushed her down on the bed and proceeded to climb on top of her. He grabs her by her throat real tight peering down on her.

"You think you can come into my party and play me bitch? It doesn't work like that.

You're my bitch, and I'm your man, and you will respect that." He says, squeezing Tamara's throat tighter. She struggled for air as he squeezed harder.

"Bitch, don't you ever disrespect me again. Especially in my own home. Next time I will beat your muthafucking ass. You hear me bitch?" He says, shaking her with his hands still wrapped around her throat. She nodded yes as the tears started spilling down her face.

He finally released her allowing her to get up. She let out a few coughs trying to get her breath back. He never took his eyes off her. It was like he was up to something. He gently pushed her back on the bed, mounting her again.

"Now that I think about it, you're my girl. That means I own everything. I think, it's time you showed me what's going on down here." He says, rubbing her crotch area.

She started sniffing in fear. This was turning into a nightmare. This is not how she envisioned, losing her virginity. Before he could get started, he heard somebody knocking on his door.

"Open this door boy. What did I tell you earlier? I

said no girls in your room. Now open this muthafucking door." His Mom says.

Tyrin quickly jumped off Tamara and straightened himself out.

"You better not say shit either. Dry those fucking tears."

She wiped the tears from her face as his Mom banged on the door.

"Boy unlock this fucking door now. You got two seconds before I kick this muthafucka in.

I'm not playing nigga."

"I'm coming Mom, I'm coming."

Tamara just wanted to get out of here. She knew she was done with him after today. Only

problem was that Tyrin didn't get that memo. She was gonna find out the hard way, that she would never be able to escape him.

The following evening

Tamara's Mom was out with one of her many

different boyfriends, so Tamara once again was home alone. Flashbacks of the party remained in her thoughts. She couldn't believe that she was seconds away from being raped in a house full of people. She tried to tell her Mom.

about it when she came home. She couldn't even avoid Tyrin knowing where she lived, because he had walked her home the day they talked at Fresh Grocers. Plus, her Mom was too faded to even listen. While she was watching television, Tracy had called. Tamara was a little pissed with her so

called best friend. She answered the phone giving Tracy a piece of her mind.

"Damn bitch, really? It took you a whole day to finally call me?"

Tracy sighed on the phone.

"Oh my God, stop being so dramatic. Don't be mad at me because his Mom stopped you from getting your little cherry popped."

Tamara couldn't believe what Tracy just said to her. She was more pissed now, more than she was when she saw her number pop up.

A Blood Stained love

"Fuck you bitch, that muthafucka tried to rape me last night, after he threatened to beat my ass. But I guess you don't see nothing wrong with that."

It was a brief period of silence on the phone before Tracy finally responded.

"Funny, didn't look like you were being forced to go upstairs with him. It looked like you were a willing participant. I didn't see him dragging you, or you are kicking and screaming.

You know sometimes you can be really dramatic."

Tamara had to take a couple breaths to get herself together. She was at the point she was ready to snap.

"How would you know? The way you were all on Sean's lap with another nigga rubbing on you.

I'm surprised you didn't get tag teamed with your smutty ass. You ain't shit but a fucking slider."

Tracy was a little caught off guard by her friend's comment.

"Oh, so now I'm a slider because you think I fucked the nigga. You know what? Fuck you bitch.

A Blood Stained love

I'll holla when you get some sense."

Tamara disconnected the call before Tracy could finish talking. She tossed her phone on the couch. Two minutes later she got a knock at the door.

"Who is it?"

There was no response. They had no peephole, so she asked again.

"Who is it?" She asked once again.

Again, no response. She took a deep sigh as she opened the door. When she opened the door,

she was surprised to see Tyrin standing on her steps. She tried to shut the door, but he stuck his foot between the doors. It was nobody outside, so nobody knew he was here.

"Please, can I talk to you for a second? I won't stay long. Just give me a second."

"One. There, your second is up, now please leave."

That pissed him off. He used his shoulder pushing the door back knocking her to the floor.

He quickly rushed in shutting the door behind him.

He then locked the door so nobody could come in. What she didn't know was, he had been watching her house and knew her Mom wasn't

home. She crawled away from him on her knees. He gripped her around her waist picking her up.

She tried to scream, but he put his hands around her mouth to muffle her. He tossed her on the couch and began to assault her. He had his hand around her throat, while he punched her in her face several times with his other hand.

"Yeah bitch, I told you, I own you muthafucka. Who the fuck do you think you're playing with, you stupid bitch?" He says giving her a few kidney shots.

She tried hard as fuck to fight herself free, but he was too strong for her. She tried to swing at him, but he was blocking all her efforts.

"Oh, you like it rough I see. I see how you do. I like it rough to bitch."

He then unloads four to five hard jabs to her face. Blood was flying out of her mouth.

"Yeah bitch, I told you. I muthafucking told you." He

says, as he goes from punching her to now slapping her all in her face. He then tries to finish what he started at his house. He unzips his

pants pulling his dick out. She knew she had to move quick before he could finish what he was trying to start. He tries to force her shorts off, but she wasn't gonna make it easy for him. With

everything in her, she gave a real hard kick to his nuts, knocking him over to the floor. She got up quickly and ran to the kitchen. He was still grunting on the floor holding his nuts. She came back in with a knife in her hand. She was not gonna be a victim.

"Fuck you muthafucka. Fuck you." She says stabbing her attacker several times.

"FUCK YOU, FUCK YOU, FUCK YOU, FUCK YOU." She says, stabbing him over and over. She was in a demonic state. Once she stopped stabbing him, she sat next to his deceased body staring at her work. She stabbed him in his ribs, stomach, face and neck. She had blood all over her, along with

her busted lips and swollen eyes. She looked at

herself in the mirror ashamed of the reflection she was looking at. She slowly slid down the wall in tears. She cried her heart out. As bad as she felt, she was glad this nightmare was over. She then slowly got up and walked back into the living room.

She frowned her face in disgust looking at the piece of shit, dead in her living room. She picked up her phone placing a call.

She waited a few seconds waiting for the person on the other end to pick up. She tried to get her breathing together as the person on the other end responded.

"911, what's your emergency?"

THE END.

A Blood Stained love

A Blood Stained love

A Mutilated Soul

MzSheriBaby

"Why does he keep doing this to me?" Mariela Lopez whispered aloud. She wiped her tear-stained eyes. Touching her nose, she winced at the sight of blood on her hand. She was sitting on the bathroom floor, she felt like all the strength she had left her body. Her abdomen hurt so bad. Her arms were so heavy from all the blows that hit her. Her head was aching badly. Her vagina and anus felt like they were on fire. Her boyfriend, Raymond, had just brutally raped her. Not before punching her like he was Floyd Mayweather. All of this was because she rejected his sexual advances. It did no good because he got his way all the time anyway.

"I love him so much." She sighed as she attempted to get up. "Shit." She moaned in pain.

She knew she couldn't stay on the floor too much longer. Raymond had left after the violent attack. She knew he would be back and that he would want dinner as well as more sex. Not only was she concerned about Raymond, but her kids were coming home from school soon. She just couldn't let them see her like this. She couldn't get to the mirror. If she looked like how she felt, she knew she looked horrible. She had no idea what she was going to tell her children.

A Blood Stained Love

Eric and Erica were the light of Mariela's eyes. Raymond was not their father, but he made sure that the kids wanted for nothing. He was the one who paid for them to attend a prestigious private school with a $50,000 tuition cost. He paid for everything. If he was to leave, she knew that her life would be rough. She knew what it was like to be poor, and she just didn't want to go back to it for the sake of her kids.

"How did things get to be like this?" she wondered as she slowly made her way to her feet. Looking in the mirror she started to cry. Her eyes were bruised, and her nose had blood leaking from it. Her hair was a mess. She grabbed a washcloth and turned the water on. As she applied the rag to her nose, she shook her head in disbelief. As much as she couldn't stand the abuse, she couldn't stand not having the means to take care of her children. As an undocumented immigrant there was only so much that she could do to take care of her children. She could not apply for food stamps, Medicaid, or public assistance because she was afraid to be deported. When her husband Julio was alive, she didn't have to worry about a thing. He was the perfect husband. Just like Raymond, Julio made sure his family wanted for nothing. He made decent money as a construction worker.

Everything was good in her life until she got the worst news. The love of her life, her partner and best friend was gone, never to be seen or heard from again. The cops knocking on her door scared the shit out of her. She couldn't fathom what they wanted with her. But the fear was already in her. When they started talking all she heard was Julio. She spoke English fluently. She knew they were telling her husband was dead.

"No mi amor!" She screamed. The cops were telling her she had to go to make an identification. She kept saying no. Eventually they were able to reach his brother Edgardo. Mariela sunk into a deep depression after the death of her husband. She never felt good again until she met Raymond. Things were great in the beginning and now she feels like she lives in the depths of hell every day.

"Things have got to change." She said aloud.

After cleaning her face up and taking a shower she retreated to her room to put on some clothes. Time was quickly passing. The kids would be home in an hour. As for Raymond, she had no idea. All she knew was that she better have dinner ready for him.

She had a walk-in closet with every name brand

designer you could think of. She had over 300 pairs of shoes. Raymond was good to her. Her only issue with him was that he drank too much. It was one thing to drink a beer a day, but he took it to the extreme. He drank at least 4-5 beers a day. That's what she knew about when he was home. He was a truck driver, so he could be gone for 2 weeks or more at a time. It seemed that she always made him mad. The littlest things made him upset. She just couldn't figure out what she was doing to make him so mad. So, she just started saying things like "Ok, I'll fix it" or "I won't' do it again".

Walking in the closet she took a seat on her foot stool. She sat there when she needed to do some heavy thinking. Throughout her trials and tribulations, she knew there was a God. He answered all her prayers. But for some reason when she prayed for help for Raymond, it didn't work. Raymond got worse the harder Mariela prayed.

"I don't know what to do." She whispered.

She was ready to move on mentally, but she knew she couldn't. Her body was abused, her mind was emotionally drained. She didn't know whether she was going or coming. She knew one thing though she was miserable and unhappy. Besides her kids, she didn't have any friends or family.

A Blood Stained love

Raymond made sure of that. He made sure he was the only person she needed in life.

Settling on a white t-shirt and a pair of sweatpants, she went into the kitchen to prepare dinner. Every day when he was not working, Raymond knocked her around and then disappeared. Then, he would return at nighttime wanting dinner ready and waiting for him. If it wasn't done to his liking, it ended up on the wall and she would get another beating. She shook her head. Her head was hurting something crazy. She reached her hands to massage her temples.

"I feel so old," she sighed. Going into the freezer, she pulled out a bag of chicken wings. She was going to fry chicken and make rice and string beans to go with it. When she went to the window to start washing the chicken, she took a glance out of the window. She saw a couple of females walking and talking.

"They look so happy," she whispered. Seeing them made her think of her two best friends. Rather her former best friends, Sarah and Lupita. Sarah was her friend she made from high school. One of the very few kids who didn't make fun of her hand me downs or broken English. Lupita was her sister-in-law. She loved her as if she was her own sister. Lupita was the one who took the children to the doctor and helped her sign them up for schools and camps. Things went left after Edgardo died. Then along came Raymond and that was the end of their relationship. She hadn't spoken to them since she got with Raymond. He said they were no good man hating bitches who were trying to break them up. She got tired of trying to reason with him about them. She sadly made the decision to leave them behind. She now realized that she made a very bad decision.

Taking her chicken, she seasoned and floured it. She put her grease on and started on her two side dishes. As she waited for her grease to get hot, her mind wandered to what Sarah and Lupita were up to. She hadn't seen Sarah for 2 years. When they last talked, she was getting married and having a baby. Sarah asked her to be a part of her wedding. And yet she didn't because of Raymond. The popping of the grease brought Mariela back to reality. She placed the chicken in the frying pan and turned down the heat. She walked out of the kitchen and retreated to the living room. She was so sick of looking at these four walls every day. Raymond said she didn't have to work because he made more than enough money to take care of them. She had a

A Blood Stained Love

little part time job as an office cleaner. She only worked three days a week. The little money she made was really nothing to do anything with. So, she relied on Raymond to supply her and her kids every need. However, she paid for everything she got with his rage. She loved the lifestyle that she was living. She was living the same lifestyle she had when Julio was alive, yet she was starting to hate Raymond. She had to choose between the money and her well-being. The debate played back and forth in her head. She had come up with different scenarios. She had two children to take care of. The question was how she was going to survive with no money. They were miserable when she didn't have any money. There were many days and nights they survived off of oatmeal and rice. When she had money, she was able to pay someone to pick up the children and take them to the doctor. Most of all she was afraid of being deported. She couldn't fathom being sent back home while her children stayed here. So, she put up with the abuse that was given to her just so she could give Eric and Erica the best lifestyle they ever had.

"I love money too much." She whispered.

She went back into the kitchen and got busy on making her man the perfect dinner. At 3:15 Eric and Erica came waltzing in the door. Eric was his father's twin. He was fourteen years old and very tall for his age. He had brown hair and brown eyes. He was at that age where his voice was cracking, and he thought his shit didn't stink. Mariela couldn't tell him anything, cause he thought he knew it all. Mariela was concerned with the way Eric bonded with Raymond over porn and sexual conversations. She wanted so badly to tell her son that girls weren't objects for his sexual pleasure. But whenever she objected to something Raymond said, he threatened to smack her around. He never hit her in front of the kids. But she knew they heard the hell she went through after they retired to their rooms.

Erica looked like Mariela. She was 5'2 with long brown hair. She was at the awkward teenage stage of confusion. She was trying to figure out who she was at 13 years old. And in doing so she started voicing her opinion and not listening to Mariela. Raymond hated when Erica mouthed off. He never hit her, but he would yell at her often. She hated being at the dinner table with Erica and Raymond. It was always World War 3. He would yell, she would yell, and Mariela would take the beating for her daughter's smart-ass mouth.

"Hi guys. How was school today?" Mariela asked reaching out to hug them.

"It was cool" Eric replied nonchalantly as he took off his coat.

Erica shrugged her shoulders. She hated talking to her mom about stuff. She couldn't understand why her mom allowed herself to get abused by the pig Raymond. She despised him with everything in her. Erica felt like her mom disrespected her dad by being with Raymond. Her father was the gentlest, kindest person she ever knew. And now she was forced to live with an evil, mean dog.

"Dinner is ready. You can get ready for dinner at 5:30." Mariel said as she retreated to her room. She knew that her daughter was very unhappy. She expressed her unhappiness every day. Mariela was a bit tired of it. Erica didn't complain about the MacBook, iPad Pro, iPhone XS and beats headphones she received for Christmas. She didn't complain about having all the latest fashions in her closet. So, Mariela wasn't trying to hear shit her daughter had to say when it came to Raymond. She already knew the situation wasn't ideal. But it was either this or living in the street.

Mariela strolled to her room and closed the door. She felt a panic attack coming on. Her anxiety was on 1000. She just wanted to escape the reality that she lived in. Lately her memories with Raymond were bad. The only thing that initially kept her around in the beginning was the sex and money. Now all he had to really offer her was money.

Sex with Raymond was great in the beginning, but it suddenly became like a chore. It was hard to enjoy sex when your body is being used like a rag doll. Out of all the times, they had sex the most magical was the first time. She remembers it like it was yesterday. All of the good memories she cherished in the back of her mind. There were few but they made her feel like she was one special individual.

Mariela met Raymond a little over two years ago. She was filling up her tank at the gas station. She had lost her husband a month prior. The devastation of being a widow tore her up inside. When she saw him, she just ignored him? White people scared Mariela. She knew that they weren't happy about people like herself who came to this country illegally. So, she stayed clear of them. As she headed inside to pay for her gas, he called out to her.

"Hey Pretty lady!" He said with extreme enthusiasm.

Mariela wasn't sure if he was talking to her, so she kept walking. When she got to the door, he stopped her from opening it.

"Let me get that for you." He said as he smiled at her.

"Thank you," She said softly with her head down.

"There's no need to be afraid of me. I'm a good guy," he told her.

She didn't say anything she just entered the store. Her mission was to get out of there as fast as she could. There was no way she was going to have a full-blown conversation with this white guy. She picked up a few snacks that she knew her kids liked before heading to the counter. She only had $30. She prayed that it was enough.

When she got up to the counter, she put her items down. "I have $20 worth of gas and these items."

The cashier rang up the items and Mariela nearly fainted. "Your total is $35.50."

Mariela nervously moved some of the items to the side.

"You don't have to do that. I got it." The white guy

says as he moved closer to Mariela. "Ring my stuff up with hers," he tells the cashier.

"Thank you. You didn't have to do that." She said, shyly.

"I know. I told you I was a good guy." He smiled at her.

****

She had to admit that he was cute for a white guy. But she wasn't trying to be deported because of her lust over a stranger.

But lust did get the best of her that day. It was the day that led to her being abused for the entire relationship. Her bad decisions may have kept her living the lifestyle she loved but it caused her a great deal of pain and sorrow. As she sat and reminisced about the past another moment made her smile.

After days of begging Mariela to go out with him, she finally agreed. She left the children with her in-laws and headed to go have dinner with Raymond. He wanted her to meet him at his house, then they would go to some fancy five-star restaurant. Mariela was dressed to impress with a black dress and black thigh high boots. She was nervous to be going on a date with Raymond. There was something about him that made her wonder what his intentions were. He seemed so sweet and innocent. Maybe she was just not ready to be dating. After it has been a little over a month since the passing of her husband. Either way she wanted to see what Raymond was really about. She enjoyed his conversation. Plus, it was a free dinner at a fancy restaurant. Who would be crazy enough to turn that down?!

Upon entering the house, Mariela knew she wasn't going to a restaurant. There were candles lit and roses everywhere. Raymond appeared and told her to sit at the table. The food looked delicious, but Raymond looked way better. Mariela could feel the moist juices escaping her vagina.

"You look very nice," Raymond said, attempting small talk.

Mariela didn't come for the small talk. "What do you really want from me?" She said looking him dead in the eye.

"What do you mean?" Raymond asked with confusion in his voice.

"You said you were taking me to a fancy restaurant, but yet you have dinner here on the table. So, what's for desert? Me?" She asked slyly.

Raymond still had the confused look on his face. "I didn't mean any harm, I just changed plans last minute."

Right… thought Mariela. It wasn't going to be a waste of a night though. She was going to get something more than food out of this. She walked closer to Raymond.

"Do you like me?" She asked him seductively. She placed her mouth close to his. She could smell the beer on his breath.

"Of course, I like you. I am very attracted to you." He whispered.

"Show me how much you like me," she whispered as she walked toward the couch.

Raymond was ready to tear her ass up. He didn't say anything as she continued to walk toward the couch. He was enjoying the little bounce she had in walk that made her ass jiggle.

"It is so on," he said in his head.

As soon as she was near the couch, he quickly moved toward her. He grabbed her and threw her down on the couch. She looked up at him in shock. Her face expression only turned him on more. He crawled between her thick legs and kissed her kitty cat. The more he kissed the more she squirmed. He then stuck his tongue deep into her love canal. Mariela was paralyzed by the intense pleasure she was feeling.

"Raymond," she protested. He got up and took his boxer off revealing his thick penis.

"Never mind. I'm ready" she thought. Raymond pulled her up as he sat down and sat her on top of him. He guided her soaking wet canal to his hard as a rock penis.

"Aaah! Mariela screamed instantly. Raymond lay back and allowed her to ride him like a cowgirl. Her moans got louder and louder by the second. She collapsed on his shoulder. She looked tired but he was far from finished. He slid out of her and laid her down on her stomach. Once he was in, Raymond made it a mission to have her tap out. The harder he went the louder she screamed. She tried pushing away, but he grabbed her hands and arched her back more. He knew that he wanted Mariela to be with him.

"I'm cummminng…" she moaned. Raymond hammered into her as he felt himself about to explode. He collapsed on top of her. She wiggled from underneath him.

"It would have been nice if you had let take my stuff off," she said with a sigh.

"Sorry I was thirsty for your love baby," he said, smiling at her.

"I need to talk to you about something," she said, changing the subject. Her demeanor had completely changed. He knew she was about to bring up some bullshit.

"I'm listening," he said, sitting up to give her his undivided attention.

"Can we take a shower and lay in the bed?" She said as she got up off the couch.

"Are you going to let me love you some more?" he asked, heading to the bathroom.

She followed him. "Whatever you say, Daddy."

****

A Blood Stained love

After they made love for hours Mariela told Raymond about the situation with her and her children. She was literally homeless. At the moment, they lived with her in-laws. It was a miserable place to be. She had no way to sustain taking care of her children. All her money literally went to the house and her kids' basic needs.

Raymond was ecstatic to help her out. He told her he had more than enough room and money for her and her kids. Feeling like her prayers had been answered, Mariela made the decision to move in with Raymond. It was a decision that she regretted a couple of weeks after she made it.

The first time Raymond hit her it was because she turned the tv off when he had fallen asleep on the couch. She went into the kitchen to clean up and get ready for bed. Raymond entered the kitchen shortly stumbling around.

"Who the fuck told you to touch my tv?" He growled at her as he came closer.

Mariela had her hands in the sink. When she went to turn towards him, she felt his hand hit her face. Stunned Mariela moaned out loud and held her face. She couldn't believe what just happened.

"Why did you…" Mariela never got to finish her sentence. Raymond started punching and slapping her. All she could do was put her hands up to soften his blows. When the beating stopped Mariela was dazed and confused.

"Clean this shit up and don't touch my shit again!" He yelled before exiting the kitchen.

That was the first of the many awful beatings she endured. Most over things she felt were stupid, like the remote incident. But it didn't matter. She was too far involved to just walk away. It wasn't just about the money. The fact that she was undocumented was something that Raymond held over her head. She couldn't risk being deported and separated from her children. And for that reason, she justified the bullshit she went through. She just let Raymond say and do whatever he wanted just so he could go about his business and leave her alone. She learned the hard way that he hated her nagging and questioning him.

Surprisingly dinner was better than usual. No one really talked too much. Mariela grew nervous until Raymond said, "Hey kids how would you like to spend the weekend with your grandparents?"

Mariela kept in contact with her husband's parents. She wanted her children to at least have their grandparents in their lives. She wasn't sure where Raymond was going with the conversation, so she kept her mouth shut.

Erica replied, "Sure."

"Whatever." Eric said.

"Ok, so after dinner we can drop you guys off."

Mariela still was uneasy, but she had nothing to say. She was just enjoying the peace and quiet. She was excited to be spending the weekend with Raymond alone. It may be just what they needed to make their relationship better.

****

It was supposed to be a day for just her and Raymond. He promised to take her on a nice trip somewhere. Night fall was approaching. Mariela was growing impatient. She went over to the couch and slowly nudged Raymond.

"Hey, it's getting dark outside," She whispered.

"What the fuck is wrong with you?" He snarled at her

jumping up off the couch. Mariela was scared shitless. She couldn't open her mouth to yell. His hand around her neck got tighter and tighter. She didn't know what to do or say to make him get off her neck. She said a silent prayer.

"Get your ass out of my face." He said releasing her out of his grip. He shoved her toward the room. "Just for that dumb shit your ass isn't going any fucking where!!" he screamed at the top of his lungs.

She ran to her room and closed the door. She sat on the edge of the bed and listened. She could hear him moving around. When she heard the door slam, she knew she had a spit second to make a decision. She hopped off the bed and went into the closet. She grabbed a big duffel bag and began throwing in her most prized possessions and some clothing. She left her cell phone on the bed. She threw on a hoodie and a pair of sneakers. Raymond only let her dress like that in the house. When they went out it had to be stilettos and dresses.

"Tsk I'm done with this shit!" She said, cautiously approaching the door. She cracked it open and peeped out looking in both directions. She quickly ran out the door, locked it and started down the stairs not looking back. Their

A Blood Stained love

neighbor Mrs. Richardson was out in the lobby.

"I am not in the mood for your lecture." Mariela said, shaking her head.

"You look like you saw a ghost dear. What's the matter you finally tired of that white man beating your ass." She hissed at her. "You young girls make me sick just letting these worthless men treat you any kind of way."

"I don't want to talk about this. I am on my way out." Mariela said, slowly as she approached the door.

"Just because he treats you like a piece of shit, doesn't mean you are a piece of shit. You need to leave him." Mrs. Richardson said, loudly.

"Thanks for the advice," Mariela said and pulled the door open.

When she got outside, Mariela ran like her life was on the line. She knew the extent of Raymond's rampages on her body. Someone that didn't even know her warned her that he would be the death of her. Mariela didn't want to die. "I have my whole life ahead of me," she thought. Mariela was running so blindly that she didn't realize a black car was approaching her at a fast speed until it was too late.

Boom she hit the floor. The driver got out and bent over her. "Hey are you ok." He asked with panic in his voice.

"Call Sarah. (347)966-555." She whispered before she passed out. The driver pulled out his cellphone and called the number that was given to him.

"Hello, is this Sarah?"

"Who is this?"

"There was an accident, and I was told to call you."

"With whom?

"Mmm. Hold on." He went into Mariela's bag to look for her wallet. He couldn't find it, so he described Mariela to Sarah. Mrs. Richardson came running up being the nosy neighbor that she was.

"Her name is Mariela. And she lives in this building on the 6th floor." She screamed into the phone.

"Oh my God, Mariela!! I will be right there! Where are you?" Sarah screamed. After rattling off the location of the accident, Rick Johnson called 911 and reported the accident. Rick was an accountant at a big firm. He didn't want to risk going to jail for hitting Mariela. So, he stayed with her until the police arrived.

The police arrived fifteen minutes after the call was made. At the same time two girls came running up to the scene of the accident. The police tried to hold them back but one of the girls put up a fight. "That's my friend" she screamed. She wouldn't calm down, so they let her through. The EMT's hoisted Mariela on a stretcher and prepared to load her into the ambulance. "I want to go with her," she pleaded. After Mariela was in the ambulance, Sarah was allowed to come inside the ambulance. After everyone was secured the ambulance took off.

A million and one thoughts were running through Sarah's mind. She watched as the EMT's poked and prodded with her friend's lifeless body. She didn't know whether she was dead or alive. She started crying because she wasn't as close to Mariela anymore. She wasn't quite sure why their friendship went sour. All she knew was that a man was involved. It was typical of people to get in a relationship and not have time for their friends. Sarah thought nothing of it.

Until she saw that her calls and texts were being ignored. Mariela didn't come to her wedding or baby shower. Then Mariela's number was disconnected. It saddened her to lose Mariela as a friend. After all they had been through. They have been friends since they were in school. Sarah had no idea of the abuse that Mariela had endured at the hands of Raymond. In fact, Sarah had never met him. She had heard so much about him. Everything she heard was good. She never had a reason to not accept their relationship until now.

"Do you have any idea where she got all these bruises from? It doesn't look like she got all of these from the car accident." The paramedic asked Sarah.

Sarah came closer to see what he was talking about. Mariela was covered in bruises. Sarah was studying pre-med. She could tell that some of the bruises weren't from the accident from the way they were healing. Mariela's shirt was ripped open, so Sarah pulled it off her. There were more bruises. "What the hell has happened to her?!"

"No, I have no idea about any of the bruises. She has a boyfriend and two children." Sarah said.

The ambulance stopped and the door was pulled open. Mariela was whisked away into the hospital. Sarah did not know the extent of her injuries, but she could tell her friend had suffered bad. Sarah entered the hospital and took a seat as she watched her friend be rushed to a room. She couldn't believe what was happening. "I'm going to get to the bottom of this!" She stated. Tears rolled down her eyes as she thought about her friend.

Entering the apartment around pm Raymond started calling for Mariela. When she didn't answer he began looking for her. When he entered the bedroom and noticed her cellphone and the open closet, he knew that she was gone.

"This bitch done left me!" He shouted, punching the wall. He took his anger out on everything in the room. He punched a hole in the 68' flat screen TV, he damaged all the furniture. A knock at the door stopped him.

'This better be her ass!" He forcefully opened the door ready to snatch Mariela by her neck and beat her ass but was surprised when he saw two police officers at the door.

"What the hell are they doing here?" He wondered.

"There was an accident earlier today with Mariela Lopez. May we come in." one of the officers said?

Raymond hated police and didn't want them coming into the apartment. Especially considering, he just wreaked havoc on his bedroom. He stepped outside and pulled the door behind him.

"She is my girlfriend. Is she ok" Raymond asked?

"No apparently she was running and got struck by a car." The officer replied.

"Oh my God I have to get to her." Raymond said in a panic.

"No, you can't go to see her. We need you to come down to the police station to answer some questions." The female officer replied.

Raymond couldn't stand it when females spoke with high authority. "Look I don't have time for this. My girlfriend needs me. I will come down to the station tomorrow with my lawyer."

"You need to come with us sir." she stated again.

"Look can you just tell your little partner here that I need to get to my girlfriend." Raymond said, turning to the male officer.

"Sir I understand your concern, but you can't go see your girlfriend." The officer replied.

"Why the hell not?" Raymond said, angrily.

"Your girlfriend was covered with bruises that were not from the car accident. We just want to get to the bottom of things. It is our job." The female officer stated.

"Are you insinuating that I did something to my girlfriend?!" Raymond was getting angrier by the minute.

"It is not our job to insinuate. We want to get facts. If you just come down and answer some questions this can all be cleared up."

"Let's go so I can get this shit over with and get to Mariela."

"What happened to me?" She opened my eyes and couldn't see a thing. After blinking her eyes several times, she could tell she wasn't home. "Where the hell am I?" she whispered. She tried to move, and it hurt like hell. She felt like she had been run over by a pickup truck. She felt a tube in her nose and an IV in her arm. Mariela knew she was in a hospital. The door abruptly opened, and a woman came in. She flicked on the light and came toward me. She noticed me looking at her and asked. "How do you feel now Ms. Lopez? My name is Dr. Ruben."

"Why am I here?" Mariela whispered.

"Initially police responded to a call that you were hit by a car. But after further inspection and observation it has come to be more than that. You came in here about 7 weeks pregnant and covered in bruises. Bruises not obtained from the car accident."

"Pregnant?" she whispered.

"Yes, but you lost the baby. I can't tell you how until you tell me what happened to you." The doctor responded.

"Nothing happened. It was just an accident." Mariela replied.

"This" The doctor said lifting up her arm" is not an accident. I can tell that most of the bruises you have were there before the accident. I can also tell that your nose has been broken and your eyes bruised. You can lie to me all you want but you are hurting yourself. If there is someone hurting, you then you need to tell the police." The doctor said ready to walk out of the room.

"Wait a minute did you speak to the police?" Mariela asked.

"Yes, I did. I am mandated under law to report any activity in which you are harming yourself or I believe that someone is causing harm to you." She said.

"I told you nothing is going on!" Mariela shouted.

"That's what your mouth says but your body says something else. I will return in the morning. Good night Ms. Lopez." She said walking out.

"Oh no! I am in so much trouble with Raymond! I should have never tried to escape him. He is going to kill me now!

Mariela laid back. "I have to get out of here." She closed her eyes and thought of a plan to escape the hospital and the wrath of Raymond for good.

A knock at the door startled Mariela. She slowly turned to her side hoping whoever it was would go away. She wasn't feeling up to talking to anyone. She knew she would have to face the consequences of trying to escape.

"Mariela?" She heard a familiar voice all out to her.

"Sarah," she whispered. The person came closer, and Mariela gasped. There standing in front of her was her dear best friend. She hadn't seen her in so long she had no clue as to the last time she saw her. Instantly tears started rolling down her face. Mariela nearly jumped out of her skin when Sarah touched her.

"How are you feeling?" Sarah asked.

Mariela didn't respond. She had so much to say to her dear friend but had no clue where to start. Being with Raymond, he controlled all her thoughts and actions. She didn't know who she was anymore. All she could do was cry.

Sarah took her hand and said, "It's ok. Whoever hurt you won't hurt you anymore."

Mariela shook uncontrollably. She knew the words Sarah spoke where untrue. She could go to the other side of the world and Raymond would find her and kill her. She was trapped and she knew it. She could feel the ass whipping she had coming. She just hoped that he didn't end up killing her one day.

Sarah felt like Mariela was a different person. She

didn't appear happy to see her. "What the hell is going on?" she wondered. She was tired of wondering. After she had seen the bruises on her friend, she wanted answers. She didn't want to pressure her friend today about her injuries, but she didn't like how her friend was acting. She was happy to see her, but she could tell that her presence wasn't wanted. She had no clue what she had done to Mariela.

"What happened to you?" Sarah asked.

Mariela knew that Sarah was gonna keep coming at her with questions if she didn't respond. She didn't want her to know the truth, so she embellished it. "I was in a rush to get across the street and a cab hit me."

"Ok, I got that part. How did you get all those bruises all over your body?"

"The accident," Mariela answered in a low tone. She wasn't a good liar. If Sarah continued her line of questioning, she would be forced to tell the truth.

"There is no way in hell all those bruises caused by a car. You want to try answering the question again? Sarah said with her arms folded.

"I don't want to talk about it." Mariela sighed.

A Blood Stained Love

Sarah sighed. She knew how bullheaded Mariela could be. So, she let it go. For now, she would let friends get all the rest she needed. She wouldn't let her go back to whatever was causing her harm.

****

Raymond was highly pissed. He was going to beat the shit out of Mariela. Now he was stuck in a police precinct while her ass is in a hospital bed. On his fucking dime! She was going to pay for her stupid ass stunt. In the meantime, he had to figure out how he was going to get out of the police station. He was quite sure the doctors had seen the bruises all over her body. He shook his head and prepared for the bullshit.

When Mariela woke up in the morning, she found Raymond sitting in a chair near the window. She was so startled she wanted to shit herself. "Fuck" she silently screamed.

"Good morning, Beautiful." He said, noticing she was awake. He got up and came toward her. Mariela flinched. Raymond gently rubbed her face and delicately kissed her lips. Mariela felt uncomfortable. She knew that this was an act. "This can't be real" she thought. "He is going to kick my ass something horrible."

"Good morning," she said to him nervously.

"How did you sleep last night?" He asked her. She looked up at the clock on the wall. It read 8:45am. She had finally drifted off to sleep around three am.

"I slept ok." She said.

"You hungry?" He asked her.

Mariela was starving. She hadn't eaten since she had left the house last night. "Yes I am." Raymond went over to the windowsill and brought her tray over to her. He placed it in front of her. The scent of eggs, pancakes and sausages hit her nose making her even hungrier.

"Mmm smells good," she moaned.

She picked up the fork and began to dig in. Raymond walked over to the door and closed it. Mariela didn't have a roommate which didn't work in her favor. No one was in the room to protect her from what was about to happen next.

Raymond came over to her and picked up her cup of hot water for her tea. Mariela thought nothing of it when she saw him with the cup, so she continued to eat. In the next instant she felt hot water all in her eyes and mouth. She was stunned.

"What the fuck were you thinking?" Raymond asked her calmly.

Scared to move she said and did nothing.

Raymond snatched the covers off her. "I'm talking to your dumbass!" he yelled.

"I wasn't thinking. I needed some air, so I went out and wasn't paying attention when I got hit." Mariela said in a hurry.

"If that's your bullshit story stick to the shit if the cops ever ask you to ask." He wrapped his arms around her neck. Mariela couldn't breathe or move.

"You are one stupid bitch!" Raymond yelled as he applied more pressure to her neck until she stopped moving. When she was dead, pulled the cover over her and laughed.

"I told you to stop fucking playing with me. You made me do this to you." He turned and walked out the room closing the door behind him.

A Blood Stained love

A Blood Stained love

Go be Healed

Nina Monica

A Blood Stained Love

I never had the typical life. I have no loving mother and father. Where was this picket white fence most speak of? Where was my dog and loving family, where was the table with all the food and hugs and words of grandeur? My life wasn't bad from 11 and under it's the latter that changed me.

I grew up in the Southeast of the nation's capital, Washington DC. My grandparents raised me in a loving home. We went to the farms when the weather was nice. I still see the hills of red from the strawberry farm. I remember the helicopter pad in the distance. I remember the smell of the fresh air and the freeness of my spirit. My grandmother took extra special care of me in the morning time before I went to school. She made sure my hair was neatly combed and my face was shiny. I still hear my Aunt's voice saying, "Stop putting all that grease on that baby face". I didn't care because I looked shiny and smelled clean. My grandfather was an extraordinarily strong, handsome tall black man. His skin was dark, and he never really smiled. He was firm in everything he said, but he was caring deep inside and so highly intelligent. He taught me how to draw and write in script in kindergarten. He made sure I was ahead of all my peers. The time passed and my grandparents grew older. Sickness set in. My grandfather passed first and that hurt. It changed me forever. During my grandfather's funeral I met my biological mother. Very foreign to me, my entire life I didn't know her. No visits and maybe one call I can recall and one letter that I can remember. I found out so many truths at a really young age. My grandmother wasn't my grandmother, the woman who raised me was simply my grandfather's girlfriend. To me that made her brave. She willingly raised a child she had no blood relation to. She didn't have any children of her own. My mother broke this news to me hastily though. She immediately wanted me to leave the woman who had raised me and move in with her all the way in New York City. I dodged her the first time and was hidden at a relative's house. No one wanted me to leave. All I knew was my Q street friends in Washington D.C. Finally, the day came where I had to leave. I had to go, I had to be taken away with a stranger that claimed to be my mother. I never saw my grandmother again. That goodbye was forever. She later died that year. I know it was from a broken heart. She had no one.

    I remember arriving in New York City, I remember the smell of the subway and streets. We arrived home finally. I recall getting off the Q111 and looking up at these

A Blood Stained love

tall buildings. There was my new home, Baisley Park Houses in Jamaica Queens, New York. The piss in the elevator, the rough looks, the new family I didn't know. I was introduced to my siblings as their older sister which wasn't easily received because they didn't know who I was, and I didn't know them either and there I met the man who scarred me for the rest of my life. My now stepfather. He was brutal, he sat me down with no love or hesitation and told me the house rules. He was stern but a different type than my grandfather. It was something different. I couldn't figure it out at 11 years old. I noticed whatever he said my Mom did. I wasn't in love though as I had watched between grandma and grandpa. That night he beat my sister with a wooden clothing dryer until it broke. That was the signal in my head this wasn't home. I didn't want to be here. The abuse became worse. He beat my mother one day because he had asked for cereal and she gave him a bowl of cereal, but it wasn't the kind he wanted. He meant oatmeal and she gave him King Vitamin with milk in a bowl. I remember her crying. It was a hard sound in my ear drums. I still hear her cries in my head to this day. He took a special liking to me though. A perverted liking. My mother had a horrible vision of me. She told many, I was sleeping around with men when

A Blood Stained love

I was in DC including my neighbor's husband to this day, I have no idea where that came from. I wasn't even sexually active.

My stepfather invited me in the room one day and told me to have a seat. He explained since I wanted to be fast and having sex, he had to show me the proper way of doing this. He told me in some countries that's how they taught their young women about sexual encounters. He made me watch him and my mother's sexual encounter. I sat there, confused. He attempted to invite me, but I froze and told him 'no', firmly. My mother also told him no as well. I was excused from the room. The sexual encounters didn't stop there only this time he didn't include my mother. He would touch me every time my mother walked out that door. I hated being home. He was physically abusive to me as well. He would hit me if I didn't do as he said. I wanted this nightmare to end. I wanted someone to come help me but there was no one. I didn't know anyone; I didn't have anyone. No friends, no family. I was introduced to family members but what was I supposed to say to them? I didn't know I could trust them. I attempted to tell my counselor in my school and that made it worse. ACS was called and came to my home and when they left, I was left too. To deal with the repercussions of putting people in our business. I was chased around the kitchen because my stepfather wanted to kill me. I ran out the door finally and down the stairs. I ran so fast and didn't look back. I didn't even know whether he was behind me. I just knew I had to get away. I was looked at as a fast behind girl to all the nosy people in the projects, I was known as being defiant and disrespectful. I wish the people that were being nosey were nosey enough to find out what was happening to me and help. I needed help. I needed a rescue, a savior, a safe space. I didn't have one. Where was I to go? I had to eventually return home. My mother scolded me and said how bad I was and how I wanted her man. I had ruined her relationship. She told me it was my fault he wanted me because I would wear short shorts and t-shirts in the house. I was now the black sheep. I hated who I was. I wanted to die. Who knew I existed anyway? I had no friends. No one to turn to.

I remember one day when enough was enough. My mother had gone to the store a few blocks down, and I was left with my stepfather in the house alone. He attempted to touch me, and I told him no. He cursed me so bad. He said, "I never wanted your little ass, what would I do with you?" He flipped the script. His abuse towards my mother became worse. He abused her until one day she decided to get him arrested. He was like a monster. She was so scared. We had to sleep with the couch in front of the door in case he attempted to come back. The courts however told her she couldn't just put him out. She had to allow him in because he was on the lease. Right then and there she decided to defend me in the cold hallways of the courthouse. She blurted out in front of hundreds of people "He is molesting my daughter". To me every head turned, time slowed. Everything was in slow motion. I remember what I had on, a black sundress with flowers, I think those flowers melted, my vision became blurry. The smell of the courtroom became strong. I could smell the wood and paper. I was taken to the side by a court officer and asked was this true? Now we had another problem, ACS was back in our lives, I still had to tell my story again. It was just too late now, I didn't care. My mother only mentioned this because it would benefit her from being abused again It wasn't for my benefit. The damage was done already.

    I eventually found love elsewhere, in the streets of Southside Queens. I thought I knew something about boys. Until I ran across a set of brothers who took advantage of me. One pretended he liked me enough to get me to sleep with him and then he invited his brother and friend to join him. I screamed, once again no one heard me. No one thought to be nosey enough to help me. I ran into those brothers later in life and nothing changed. They thought it funny, they thought they had accomplished something. They laughed at me right there in the mall in front of lots of people. I was beyond embarrassed though. It was like I was cold; I think back on this incident and they probably should have been in jail. They had to have been much older than me. I found myself in uncomfortable situations often. It was fear that struck me every time. Do I give in or do I take flight? Most often I gave in to prevent myself from sleeping in the project hallways because I had nowhere else to go. My mother didn't care about my whereabouts. She would lock me out at 6 in the afternoon some days. People thought I was just wanting to be in the streets. So many doors were being closed in my face. I finally found love in a church. I had a church home. I used to go to church so I wouldn't have to be uncomfortable in the house. I felt a freedom when I was in the church house. I remember one morning I was locked out all night and wandered the streets. I walked up and down Guy Brewer Blvd, to Sutphin and back. I had nowhere to go. I walked by my church and saw the doors

A Blood Stained love

open and I realized they were having 6 a.m. prayer breakfast. Finally, I had somewhere to go and clean up and eat. I hadn't eaten since school the day before. I tell these stories with the remembrance of how young I was. I was no older than 14 years old. I am a mother of 2 beautiful young girls, and I couldn't imagine being able to sleep without them in the house for days. At 15 I was in a relationship with a guy who I know without a doubt cared for me, but I was too young to be in such an adult situation. We had our own basement apartment together. We used to have so much fun. I found myself pregnant though. I didn't even realize I was until well into my pregnancy. I didn't realize anything different about my body. I didn't even realize if you missed your period you could possibly be pregnant. I used to hang out at the community center which had a clinic in the building. I went there often.

  They had different projects for me to be a part of, like the National Council of Negro Women. I went there for relief from my home. I found out during a regular appointment I was having a baby in less than 4 months. I had no stomach, no morning sickness, nothing. There I was shy of 16 with a baby. I still went to school up until the day my water broke. I was still somehow trying to be responsible

A Blood Stained love

or what I knew to be responsible. Still, I faced so many uncertainties. My mother really didn't want me then. She didn't want me to live with her. I was turned away so many times. Where was I going to live with my baby? I remember sleeping on the bench in front of my building on the basketball court. I was hanging out with some friends and I pretended I was chilling but I had nowhere to go. I remember feeling like I wanted to give up and I didn't deserve to be a mother to this cute little baby boy. I never gave up though I just learned how to make ends meet. I found my love for money in the clubs. I went with a friend one night and watched her how she made her money. The next night I tried it as well. I made almost $1000 just dancing in front of a couple of strangers. I didn't even get naked. This was it, put on a sexy outfit and bam money falls from the sky. Yep, I am with it. I remember my mother watching my son some nights for me. I would give her $50, a pack of cigarettes and a 2-liter Pepsi. I still wonder where the hell did, she think I worked at?

My life as a dancer was fun but dangerous. I watched beautiful women turn to men and drugs. I saw my homeboys turn into pimps. I Thought I was living the life though. I had money, and attention. Something I wasn't getting from home. That was extremely dangerous though for a young girl. I wasn't even 18 yet and here I am caught up in this world of making fast money. Those things stuck with you though. I grew a hustler's mentality. I knew I never wanted to be without. I never wanted to fall short. Some of those things I still live by but now I know I can't be out making fast money and showing my body to men for a living.

    I carried those things with me even up to my mother's death. She held a gripe against me for the rest of her life. I carried those things into relationship after relationship. I searched for my perfection. I was scared, I needed validation for everything. I don't trust easily; I was insecure, and I thought when things went wrong in my relationships it was because they got what they wanted sexually.

    I am glad I was able to come out of each situation safely. However, many days I get caught up in those thoughts. Funny thing is, a simple I am sorry would heal the surface of the wounds I carry. Not being realistic and pretending you didn't hurt someone can be detrimental. Some people don't get through things like me. Some people never heal in any sort of form. Some people turn to a different life because they don't know anything else. I am sorry sister if he or she didn't apologize. I am sorry brother for the things you went through. And everyone pretended they didn't happen. Don't carry on alone, Find help. BE HEALED on purpose. I love you.

A Blood Stained love

Nightmare
Partie un

© K. Watson

Quincy watched Riley lift her eyebrows in surprise and frown slightly. Then, her eyes rolled back into her head and she slumped against him. Gently, he lowered her to the floor, then stepped over her. Quincy grabbed her keys and went out to her truck to gather his things. After he reentered the office building, he locked the office door behind him, turned off all the lights leaving only Riley's small desk lamp on.

Months of planning were finally paying off. He arranged the cushions and rolled the unconscious woman on to them. After slipping off her high heeled pumps. He began to unbutton the tiny pearl like buttons on her blouse. Slowly, inch by inch revealing her black lace bra, and her breasts before slipping her arms out of it. The pulling it off the rest of her off her. He then moved her slightly to her side so he could unzip the back zipper and pulled her skirt down off of her body. Quincy sat back and admired Riley's half naked body. Her large breasts were securely encased in her black lace bra. Running his finger across the matching lace panties and down her toned thigh, he relished the feel of her old fashion garters and silk stockings.

Then he released her breasts from their lace prison and unhooked her garter and began to roll it and her stockings off. Standing, he quickly stripped down naked and knelt beside Riley. Something was missing. Looking around at the scattered clothes on the floor he grabbed her pumps and slipped them back on to her feet. Taking a moment, he enjoyed her laying there helpless. Stroking himself he smiled he before he reached for the bag he had brought in and grabbed the needle he had pre-drawn then administered just enough antidote to rouse the woman but not wake her fully.

Riley's eyes fluttered open as she slowly came to, trying to remember where she was. Everything was so fuzzy, and her head throbbed dully. She tried to raise her hand, but her limbs felt like lead. Moaning, she tried to turn her head, but her body would not obey her. A face came into view and leaned over her. Through the haze in her brain, she thought she recognized Quincy. Shifting her focus, she came to the realization that he was shirtless.

"Q," she mumbled.

"Shhhhhh...it's ok Riles. It's just a dream," was his whispered reply.

"No, Q, where are we? Where's your shirt?"

"Shhhhhhh…it's ok. I'm going to make it all better.

Quincy could feel the predatory smile spread over his face as he leaned over and kissed her. Startled, Riley realized to her horror she was naked and lying on a cushion of some sort in her office at work.

Quincy broke the kiss then spread her legs and lowered himself on her. Her brain reeled as he slowly started to kiss and lick her neck making his way down to her breasts.

Quincy was in heaven. Riley's skin tasted so good, salty sweat mixed with the fear that was practically oozing out of her. He arms twitched and her legs moved feebly as if she was trying to make an escape, but he knew that she had enough of the shot he had given her that her thought process wasn't a hundred percent clear leaving room for doubt and that her body was at his mercy. Leering at her breast he lowered his mouth to her nipple and began to suck.

Riley's mind reeled as Quincy sucked her hardening nipple. She tried to raise her arm and push him off then to move her legs to roll over and throw him, but her limbs were useless. Her nipples, however, had a mind of their own under the onslaught of Quincy's mouth.

"Q," she mumbled. "Stop please this isn't right."

Quincy lifted his head and smiled at her. "Shhh," he whispered, "It's just a dream, Riles. You know I'd never hurt you."

Smiling that predatory smile again attacking her breast, licking and sucking pleased to hear the low moan escape her lips. Releasing her nipple, he kissed and nibbled his way down until he reached her panties.

Riley tried to concentrate. Quincy was her best friend, her MARRIED best friend. She thought of him as a brother. He had come by the office to pick up some equipment for his job tomorrow and stopped in to say goodbye. She remembered getting up to let him out when he called her name, she turned around almost bumping into him when she felt an odd stinging sensation in her right buttock then everything went black. Now here she was lying in her office unable to move. Is it possible?" she thought, my BEST friend was going to rape me? This couldn't be real. Maybe she was dreaming. But this felt so

A Blood Stained love

real. Riley's thoughts snapped back to the present as she felt Q grasp the waist of her panties, slide them down over her rear and off her legs.

Quincy moaned in lust as her curly dark bush appeared. He put his face in her honey pot and inhaled. He trailed his finger along her folds and slowly slid it into her.

"You are so wet Riley," his raspy voice slurred. "So wet. I can't wait to taste you."

Riley gasped.

"Q," she rasped. "Please don't. You are my best friend. This isn't right."

"Shhhhhh…. it's just a dream Riles," Quincy mewled, "Just a dream remembers."

Quincy smiled and licked his finger. He immediately began to suck her pearl, getting a deep moan out of Riley. Trailing his tongue along her folds he licked and sucked trailing his tongue in lazy circles around then flicking her pearl. He plunged in one then two fingers while he sucked her pearl like a baby sucking a pacifier. Her low throaty moan told him she was close. Attacking her pearl again, he was rewarded as she cried out weakly and her sweet cream flooded his mouth.

"So good Riles…. You taste so good. Better than I imagined. Do you know how long I've wanted to taste you? From the first day, I walked in this office."

Reluctantly he moved his head from between her legs and positioned himself on top of her, his weight resting on his elbows.

"Q stop please you are my best friend," Riley half mumbled half begged. She moaned softly as he traced her folds with the head of his manhood. A lone tear pooled in her eye, then trailed down her temple into her hair.

Quincy stopped and kissed the trail. "Shhh, riles…don't cry. It's ok. I'm not hurting you. I just want to make you feel good. How long has it been since a man made you feel this good," he whispered?

"Q, please-" Riley cried but the protest was cut off as Quincy again kissed her; sucking on her bottom lip while he slid his large manhood into Riley's wet tunnel.

"So tight," Quincy moaned, his lust taking over. "God Riles, I wish I'd know how tight you were, I'd have done this long ago."

Riley moaned as she was invaded. He was so big. Why was this happening? Quincy had never been anything but a gentleman. They had bonded almost instantly when he came in for the interview laughing and talking like old friends. He was always there for her when she was upset. This is a nightmare…a terrible nightmare. Why can't I wake up?

Giving himself a minute to adjust to the velvety tightness that engulfed him, Quincy licked and kissed the side of Riley's neck then up to her ear where he playfully nipped her earlobe, before he started to slowly piston back and forth. Grabbing her leg, he hiked it up giving himself better access to her so he could go deeper, her moan was his reward.

"God Riles you are so beautiful," he whispered. "My beautiful Riles you are mine at last. I've wanted you so long. Wanted to taste you and feel my dick going deep in you. Ugh…I don't want to cum too quick, but I'm not sure how long I can hold off, you are so warm and wet."

Riley shuddered at his words. She was repulsed and scared, but her traitorous body was so turned on to what he was doing to her. She felt her orgasm building and prayed it would be enough to finish him off so this nightmare would end. "Nightmare, I'm home in my bed having a terrible nightmare."

Quincy moaned as her muscles tightened around him as she started to cum.

"Yes, baby that's it. Milk my dick baby, cum all over it."

Riley moaned as the orgasm tore through her but to her horror, Quincy kept going. He seemed to get harder and go faster to bring her to the edge this time but then he slowed down and stopped right before she toppled over.

"No Riles, not yet" he whispered. "I want to hold off on this one. I've waited so long I want to feel you just a little longer."

Frustrated Riley felt the tears welling. Why wouldn't this end, why couldn't she wake up"?

Quincy wiped away the tears that spilled out of her eyes.

"Shhhh Riles," he whispered. "It's ok, beautiful. Q will make it all better."

Slowly he began to move in and out again. Driving into her, again and again, making her moan as the tightening began then crying out weakly as she came around his massive manhood.

"Yes," he almost shouted as he finally gave in and exploded painting her insides with his hot seed.

Panting he collapsed on top of her kissing her cheeks and neck.

"Oh, my Riles, my beautiful sweet sexy Riles," he whispered, wiping away the tears that still rolled down her cheeks. "Don't cry. You made me so happy. I'm so glad you are my best friend."

Rising off her he reluctantly pulled out of her and grabbed the bag with the prepared shot. He leaned over and kissed the tip of her nose before he rolled her onto her side and plunged the needled into her hip. Smiling that lascivious smile, he watched her eyes roll back in her head and she slipped into unconsciousness.

Riley's eyes snapped open, and she sat up gasping for

air. Scanning the room her eyes darted around taking in the surroundings, her heart hammering in her chest. When she realized she was in her bed in her home she began to relax. She looked down touching the soft blue nightgown she always wore and touched it letting the soft texture calm her further.

"A dream... No, a nightmare," she whispered wrapping her arm around herself and shivering. "Just a terrible nightmare."

Ripping the covers back, she sprang out of bed, and practically ran to the bathroom, straight to the shower, stripping off her nightgown and panties along the way. Turning on the shower full blast, she relaxed as the warm spray washed the nightmare away.

Feeling better, she wrapped a towel around herself. She grabbed the phone and hit the speed dial.

"Hello," Quincy's sleepy voice sounded over the phone.

"Q, its Riles. Sorry to call you so early, especially on a workday when Olivia and the kids are out of town. But I had the worst nightmare last night. I just needed to hear your voice."

Quincy rolled over and smiled his evil smile. "Aww Riles," he said. "You know it's ok to wake me up. I'm your best friend after all. Tell me all about it. Q, will make it all better."

A Blood Stained love

Nightmare 2

Deuxième Partie

© K. Watson

Riley shook herself and stared at the computer screen in front of her and tried to concentrate. Something bad had happened to her, and that Quincy had something to do with it.

Quincy acted the same. Jovial, cordial, respectful of their friendship and his marriage, but something was off. There was something sinister behind his eyes.

Riley took a sip of her juice and cringed. The raw cranberry juice that she was drinking had a kick to it, but it was helping to flush her body out. She was still having black outs and missing time. She was still jumping at shadows, but the sluggishness and dry heaving was subsiding.

Riley tried to snap herself back into reality and again tried to concentrate when a knock on her door made her jump.

Quincy stood there smiling his usual thousand-watt smile, but something was off about it and Riley shivered.

"You ok, Riles?" Quincy asked, crossing the room his eyebrows knitting together in concern. He frowned and crossed the room to stand at her desk.

A Blood Stained Love

Riley looked up at Quincy and for the first time, she felt a flicker of fear. Pure instinct kicked in and she leaned back in the chair trying to put as much space between them as she could.

Quincy noticed the subtle change in her body language.

"What's the matter Riles"?

"N--nothing," Riley stuttered. "I think I'm just coming down with something."

Quincy reached across the desk, but Riley drew away from him like he was made of fire.

"I need some air," Riley all but shouted as she pushed back from her desk and ran out of her office.

Riley raced out of the front door and doubled over gasping for breath. Quincy and several others ran out to her.

"Riles, what is it? What's wrong?"

Quincy grabbed Riley by the shoulders and looked intently into her face. As soon as he touched her Riley had a vibrant flash of memory. Quincy was on top of her, inside her, forcing himself on her. Riley looked at Quincy's face and saw a smile of pure evil, then her eyes rolled back in her head and everything went black.

Riley opened her eyes then shut them rapidly. She squinted trying to block out the harsh light. Little by little she opened her eyes and looked around. Unsteadily, she raised her hand and caught sight of the IV in her hand.

Slowly she scanned the stark white room, machines beeped steadily that monitor vitals next to her bed and IV stand. She realized she was in the ER. A chill ran through her from the cold air, and she drew the blanket up around her shoulders and shivered.

Movement from the corner of her eye caught her attention and she turned her head in time to watch the nurse enter her room.

"Miss Edwards, how are you feeling"?

"Confused" Riley croaked as the nurse made a note in her chart.

"I'm sure you are, and probably a little scared. You gave everyone a huge scare. Do you remember what happened?"

A Blood Stained love

Riley shook her head trying to clear the cobwebs, "I was at work and my friend Q came in my office, and suddenly I felt sick, and I ran outside for some air then everything went black."

The nurse pulled out a handheld device out of the pocket in her scrub top and passed it over Riley's forehead.

"The doctor will be with you in just a moment to talk to you but from what it looks like you had a panic attack and fainted. Have you been especially stressed or ill lately?"

"I've been feeling sort of strange since last Friday. It's funny because I don't remember driving home that night and I've felt sluggish, been dry heaving and having crazy nightmares."

The nurse nodded then picked up a chart that was on the small tray table and made some notes.

"I'll be sure to tell the doctor. Meantime you lay back and try to rest. "

Riley closed her eyes and tried to relax. Images started swirling around behind her eyelids.

Flash… Q looking down at her with a vile smile on

his face.

Flash…Stabbing pain in her right hip.

Flash…Q on top of her.

Riley gasped and sat up just as the doctor entered the room.

The doctor crossed the room, placing a calming hand on her shoulder.

"Miss Edwards, I'm Doctor James. It's ok you are safe," the doctor said in a quiet voice.

Riley looked around trying to shake, the feelings of dread that were mentally bombarding her.

"What just happened Miss Edwards"?

Riley stared at the doctor. She was a short woman with salt and pepper hair and olive skin. Her white coat rustled as she pulled a chair close to Riley's bed and patted her shoulder to get her to calm down.

"It's all so jumbled," she gasped and pulled away from the doctors' touch.

Withdrawing her hand, the doctor sat and quietly.

"The nurse said that you have experienced some lost time and feeling strange and sluggish since last week. What do you remember?"

Riley took a shaky breath then rubbed her arms and tried to focus herself.

"I remember being at work, my best friend Q came in for some equipment that was left for him for a job. We talked for a minute and then he hugged me. The next thing I remember was waking up in my bed."

"You also told the nurse that you've been having nightmares. Do you remember them?"

Riley looked down and whispered, "It's like flashes of my best friend drugging and raping me."

"Is it possible?"

"No Q would never hurt me; he's happily married and has never been anything but kind and respectful."

"Miss Edwards, have you ever heard of acquaintance rape?"

"Well, yes but … he's not that kind of guy."

"Miss Edwards, perpetrators of acquaintance rape can be anyone from someone the victim is dating, to a classmate, a co-worker, an employer, or family member. Even a spouse, counselor, therapist, religious official, or medical doctor. Add to this you are experiencing some possible symptoms of PTSD. I think that you should consider counseling.

Riley gaped at the doctor in stunned silence. Burning tears welled up in her eyes and streaked rapidly down he face.

Dr. James gently rubbed Riley's hand.

"I can't begin to guess how hard this must be. But I believe that something happened to you and that counseling will help you to unlock it."

Quincy lurked at the door to Riley's hospital room and listened. He could not believe his well-laid plan was coming apart at the seams. He would lose everything if she remembered.

Cursing under his breath Quincy stalked out of the hospital trying to think of a way to fix this dilemma of his own making.

Riley sat in the overstuffed chair breathing in the soft perfume of the vanilla candle. It had been a hard road, but she was finally able to admit it, Q her best friend, had drugged her and raped her.

She stared at the flickering flame and let the tears flow.

"But…I orgasmed I remember it now. Was it rape?"

Dr. Deverter peered over her old-fashioned horn-rimmed glasses and shook her head.

"Yes, orgasm is in a healthy sexual relationship a sign of pleasure. But in situations of rape, even violent rape, orgasm is a physical response. Your body responded to stimulation. That doesn't mean you enjoyed it."

"The question is what will you do now."

"I should report it, but it's been so long there is no proof. It's his word against mine and I didn't even remember until now."

"Yes, the chances of anything legally happening are slim. Just know that whatever you decide that you have my support."

Riley drove home, her head spinning. How should she handle this? Her so-called best friend and done this vile horrible thing to her.

As soon as she got home, she made a beeline for her bathroom stripping off her clothes and jumped in the shower, scrubbing her skin until it was almost raw. Her tears mingling with the water as she sobbed. When the water finally ran cold, she stumbled out of the shower and into her room, crawling into her bed without even drying off.

The next morning as Riley crawled out of bed she felt like a different person. The sadness, confusion and doubt that had plagued her was gone and a decidedly tougher Riley remained. Staring at her reflection in the mirror she resolved to end it once and for all.

Quincy watched Riley as she marched into the building her spine ramrod straight. There was something in her stance and the grim look on her face. He steered clear of her since she started therapy, but he sensed that the situation had to come to a head soon.

Riley stared at the computer screen. She sensed someone at her door and looked up, then exhaled her blood turning to ice water in her veins. Quincy stood at her door.

"Hey, Riles, how's it going," he said casually.

Riley stiffened her eyes narrowing to slits, "Mr. Anderson, please come in. We need to talk."

"Why so formal Riley?

Before the thoughts registered in her brain, Riley pushed back from her desk and charged across the room. She stood in from of Q for a brief second before she reached up and backhanded him.

"I remember everything," she hissed. "I trusted you. I would have trusted you with my life. How could you do that to me? How could you betray me like that?"

She raised her hand to slap him again, but he caught her wrist.

"What are you talking about Miss Quinn?" Quincy said narrowing his eyes. His voice dipped with contempt as he looked down at the woman in front of him, his voice cold and unfeeling like he was speaking at a stranger and not the woman he called his best friend.

"You raped me "

"You're crazy."

"Am I?"

"Prove it."

"You know I can't, but I can make enough of a stink to make your life miserable."

Quincy stared at Riley for a long moment then released her wrist and walked away. He walked down the hall and out of the front door to his truck where he stood for a minute trying to wrap his brain around what had just happened. His carefully laid plan had disintegrated. He knew that she couldn't prove anything, but she was right, she had been there for years and was well respected and liked by everyone. The accusation alone could seriously damage his standing in the company and possibly effect other job prospects.

Slowly Riley sank to the floor breathing hard. She felt a panic attack trying to start but she took some deep breaths and forbade herself from crying. Slowly the urge disappeared, and she rose and marched to the head office.

"We need to talk," she said to her startled boss.

At the same moment Quincy took one last look at the front doors of the building he had worked at for the last few years then, got in the truck, and drove off. He knew that his life would be over, but he also knew how he could end things on his terms Riley and the rest be damned.

Turning the key in the ignition, he slammed the truck into gear and tore out of the parking lot leaving a trail of rubber. Riley and the boss looked up in time to watch open mothed as the truck peeled out and into the street.

Ten minutes later, he drove into the back of a tanker truck at eighty miles an hour and was killed instantly in the explosion.

La Fin

Authors note: This was a work of pure fiction. If you or someone you know is the survivor of a sexual assault, please call the National Sexual Assault Hotline at 1-800-656-4673. You can get help and all calls are confidential.

A Blood Stained love

A Blood Stained love

www.ingramcontent.com/pod-product-compliance
Lightning Source LLC
Chambersburg PA
CBHW070910160426
43193CB00011B/1416